Praise

Dr. Rainer's exceptional book *Life After Loss* has the rare potential of becoming a valued resource not only for the professional community but also for those they serve. His perceptive and insightful guides for journeying through the process of grief captures the reader in a rare combination of existential and applied interventions that exquisitely invite movement in all realms, affective, cognitive, behavioral and spiritual. This integrative approach invites the reader into a transformative place of healing essential for growth following loss.

—Frieda Farfour Brown, Ph.D., Psychologist
and Author, *Crisis Counseling and Therapy*

Life After Loss is a "**must read**" for all clinicians seeking practical knowledge and information to help the grieving person. Dr. Rainer's work is not only inspirational but also an all-inclusive, clinically astute, and reader friendly exposition on the complex world of grief, loss, mourning, and bereavement. This text takes its reader on an instructional journey from historical roots to current practice. Highlights of this journey include, but are not limited to, concise definitions, grief differentiation, emotional response patterns, grief counseling, social ceremonies, multicultural implications, spiritual, legal and ethical considerations, and special issues. These highlights are complimented by poignant case examples that enhance both content and reader interest. I encourage you to take this instructional journey and enhance both knowledge and skill's application in dealing with the grieving person.

—Douglas R. Gross, Ph.D., Professor Emeritus of Counseling
and Counseling Psychology, Arizona State University

We live in an era when many want to believe that death and grief are optional. If found to be absolutely necessary, it is to be expedited as swiftly and efficiently as possible. Jackson Rainer challenges such thinking. Life After Loss offers fresh insight into the troubling process of relearning one's world in the aftermath of a significant death. Anyone grieving or working with those bereaved, needs this book.

—Harold Ivan Smith, DMIN, FT, national grief expert and prolific author,
including the best-selling *Decembered Grief*

Life After Loss

Contemporary Grief Counseling and Therapy

by

JACKSON RAINER, PH.D., ABPP

PESI
Publishing
& Media
www.**PESI**.com

Copyright © 2013 by Jackson Ranier
Published by
PESI Publishing and Media
CMI Education Institute, Inc
3839 White Ave
Eau Claire, WI 54703

Cover Design: Matt Pabich
Layout Design: Bookmasters
Edited By: Marietta Whittlesey & Kayla Omtvedt

Printed in the United States of America

ISBN: 978-1-936128-46-4

*To my friends Deidre Felton, Doug Gross,
Sr. Teresa McIntier, and Marilyn Gryte, for many
days and nights spent in collaboration and collegiality*

About the Author

Jackson Rainer, Ph.D., ABPP, is a board certified clinical psychologist and is nationally known and respected as a psychotherapist, teacher, and supervisor. In urban and rural settings, he has directed community mental health institutions and agencies, practiced psychotherapy with children, adults, couples and families, and taught in universities and professional settings for a practice life than spans more than 25 years. He currently serves as Department Head for Psychology and Counseling at Valdosta State University, Valdosta, Georgia while maintaining professional service as a consulting psychologist for psychotherapy and supervision. He is the former chair of the Publication Board for Division 29, Psychotherapy, of the American Psychological Association, is on the editorial and publication boards of seven psychology journals, and serves as a Media Representative for the APA. He specializes in work surrounding the crisis of loss due to catastrophic, chronic, and terminal illness.

Table of Contents

I

Introduction

"When someone you love dies, you don't lose her all at once; you lose her in pieces over a long time – the way the mail stops coming, and her scent fades from the pillows and even from the clothes in her closet and drawers. Gradually, you accumulate the parts of her that are gone. Just when the day comes – when there's a particular missing part that overwhelms you with the feeling that she's gone, forever – there comes another day, and another specifically missing part."

John Irving, *A Prayer for Owen Meany* (1989)

The process of grief does not change a person as much as it reveals another part of the self. While grief is a psychological burden, at the same time, it is an anchor. Grief's weight holds an individual in place, allowing the survivor to answer one of the mysteries of existence – how love imperfectly shared could have had such impact. Grief awakens the individual to the deeper beauty, sanctity, and reality of the relationship and what has been lost, and eventually to gratitude for what preceded the loss. The painful purpose of grief is to acknowledge the emptiness in the loss, remember, and take solace in what was there. In a paradoxical way, grief respects the gifts of life and love.

This book, rather than being a research-oriented review of the current state of scientific knowledge in the field of grief and bereavement, is an applied resource for clinicians wanting practical knowledge and information to help those in the presence of the death of a loved one. While grounded in the contemporary science of research and best practice, the book speaks to the common and unique experiences of loss, recovery, and integration that can clearly be understood in thematic terms.

Simply put, grief is known as the natural and typical response to loss – a universal experience that is repeatedly encountered. Loss is defined as the state of being deprived of something one has had or valued. Loss may either be physical/tangible, or symbolic/psychological. It is embodied in multiple layers of feelings and thoughts which profoundly influence behavior and belief. Grief is a psychological and sociological mindset characterizing the conflict experienced following major changes in the routine and rhythm of life. The process of grief arises and is found in loss – any loss. Moving to a new community, divorce, college bound children leaving home, and retirement are common examples of life experiences where changes due to loss are figural. In this book, the loss to be examined is death. As will be noted in various ways, all losses are characterized as behavioral changes underscored by the painful emotionality of deprivation. Grief is an unpleasant emotional experience; no one likes to feel deprived.

The processes of grief are misunderstood and easily neglected. In western tradition and culture, little room is allowed for the raw nature of the grief experience. It is often viewed as an arbitrary, unnecessary indulgence and one erroneously thought to be most effectively addressed by emotional distance or a 'pull-yourself-up-by-the bootstraps' brand of psychological toughness against its emotional tidal flows. Contemporary Western society provides little in the way of death education, particularly in the experiential understanding and appreciation of mortality. Instead, the Western world teaches the value of acquisition as an aspirational ideal. Everyone must have more of everything; emotional satiation and satisfaction are rare. Most people know and snicker at the trite colloquialism, "She who dies with the most toys wins." Appreciating emptiness and making room for silence are disregarded in our fast-paced world.

While everyone logically knows that death happens, to talk and give voice to the issues and concerns of mortality is considered rude and coarse. Polite society does not discuss anything related to letting go other than in the most culturally restrictive and prescribed ways. As practitioners know, grief can be ignored for a while, but it cannot be avoided. Grief happens as the natural response to loss. Recovering from a significant loss is neither an easy task nor one for the faint-hearted. It requires attention, a level of open-mindedness, a tolerance of emotionality and vulnerability, and a series of steps, actions, and activities to be taken toward a new way of being.

Several definitions will be used throughout this text and are worthy of clear understanding from the outset. *Grief* is defined primarily by an emotional reaction to the loss of a loved one through death. It is an internal psychological experience that also involves thought recalibration, behavioral action, and belief system changes in the presence of unpredictable, though expected shifts of affective, emotional experience. Grief researcher Kenneth Doka (2003) spoke of grief as "a type of stress reaction, a highly personal and subjective response to a real, perceived, or anticipated loss" (p. 350). Grief is understood to be a figurally affective reaction which incorporates cognitive and behavioral manifestations in its presence. It is the natural reaction to loss, though grieving individuals are known to suffer elevated risks of depression, anxiety, and other psychological disorders occurring alongside the pain of the loss. In addition, grief typically has corresponding physiological and somatic changes, including upsets in appetite, sleep, and general well-being. The constellation of symptoms varies widely from one person to another, across cultural lines, and across the course of time. Poetically, grief has been referred to as the cost paid for being able to love.

While grief is an internal experience, *mourning* is the external demonstration of grief. To mourn is to find social experience in acts expressive of grief, all of which are shaped by the practices of a given society or cultural group. Mourning is the public display of grief, including the social expressions or acts that are molded by the beliefs and practices of a religious beliefs, social tradition, and cultural custom. Mourning is observed in cohesive communities where the pain of death is shared by members having common knowledge of the deceased and coming together in various rites and rituals of the dead. In a community, those grieving are surrounded by mourners having a similar experience. The nomenclature of grief and mourning are oftentimes used interchangeably, but in truth define different clinical processes, all to be discussed throughout this book.

Bereavement is a locator term, i.e., an individual is placed and found in the state of bereavement. It is the objective situation of having lost someone significant. The focus is not on death in general, but on the loss of a particular person who has died in particular circumstances. The word bereavement has its origin in the Old English term *reave*, which means to be robbed or deprived of something valuable. In present day, it now refers to the objective circumstance and situation of having lost a significant other through death and is generally taken to include personal losses across the lifespan. The state of bereavement is associated with intense distress for most people.

In sum, "I grieve; we mourn together, and find ourselves bereaved."

The word "normal" will rarely be used in this book. 'Normal' is a highly imprecise word and implies what most people do, which is not particularly useful for a grieving individual. As will be discussed in greater detail throughout this text, the expected benchmarks of grief and bereavement vary widely. "It could be defined as an emotional reaction to bereavement, falling within expected norms, given the circumstances and implications of the death, with respect to time course and/or intensity of symptoms" (Stroebe et al., 2008, p. 6). Grief does have patterns, threads, and knits, although it is eccentric and idiosyncratic. Rather than normal, it is much more generous to refer to *uncomplicated grief* as "typical" or "natural." Grief is considered as a developmental process, one that most will encounter in an unencumbered way, congruent with individual personality, temperament, and circumstance. The majority of bereaved people will have no pathology associated with their grief, and only in a minority of cases will grief be characterized as complicated by disabling symptoms.

As will be discussed further, there is a distinct subset of people who will have significant psychological problems associated with integration of death and the impact of loss. *Complicated grief* is not a single syndrome with clear diagnostic criteria, although considerable effort is being made to derive benchmarks and indicators through objective empirical research. As noted by Stroebe et al. (2004), the pathology of grief is marked by, "...a deviation from the cultural norm (i.e., that could be expected to pertain, according to the extremity of the particular bereavement event) in the time course or intensity of specific or general symptoms of grief" (p. 7). Despite major contemporary efforts, there is no agreement regarding a definitive set of symptomatology, or for that matter, whether diagnostic criteria are necessary and useful. For clinical purposes, complicated grief can be assessed and identified as a deviation from the cultural norm in the course of time and intensity of specific or general symptoms of grief (Stroebe et al., 2008, p. 7). This definition is inadequate, since it fails to account for dysfunctionality. The issue of complicated grief demarcation continues be under a fair amount of debate, since the standard nomenclature of the Diagnostic and Statistical Manual of Mental Disorders (DSM™), now in its fifth edition, requires criteria of clinical significance for mental disorders that include the specification that the condition "causes clinically significant distress or impairment in social, occupational, or other important areas of functioning" (1994, p. 7). The discussion seems to be taking a two-pronged approach to include deviation from the cultural norm in either the time course or intensity or general symptoms of grief, and the level of impairment in social, occupational, or other important areas of functioning.

In an age when people are taught not to talk about death, this book becomes important since it lends assistance to those clinicians who need tools, techniques, and compass points to help others in the experience of grief. Practicing counselors and therapists historically have been left to fly by the seat of their clinical pants when helping grieving clients. Contemporary research teaches that stage theories of grief, which have always been highly suspect by practitioners who knew better, are outmoded. There is a great need to work in ways that have fidelity to the lived experience of clients. The book will approach the topic of grief and bereavement from an interdisciplinary point of view while maintaining a clinical, applied, and theoretical context. Principles and concepts will be made more meaningful through examples and anecdotes. Psychobabble, jargon, and excessive technicality will be limited. The language used in this book will be fairly direct and plainspoken, a directive that will frequently be suggested to clinicians working with bereaved individuals and groups. While specialized terms will be clearly and succinctly defined, death and dying will be referred to as death and dying, not "passing away" "being called home," or other euphemisms. While there is psychotherapeutic value in listening for and responding to the survivor's personal metaphors about life and death, slang and regional vernacular that create psychological distance from "death talk" will be avoided. Contemporary society tends to substitute indirect or vague words and phrases for ones considered harsh or blunt. Essentially, such words mask reality. This book seeks to avoid such a trap.

The formulation of new models of grief is helping to integrate and give direction to current research that carries fresh and useful implications for clinical practice. This book will define, explore, and illustrate these attributes, models, and skills. Death is intrinsic to human experience, yet one that contemporary society seeks to distance from and deny. In his work "The Masque of the Red Death," Edgar Allen Poe wrote of death as a mysterious stranger at a costume ball whose mask concealed his true face. The disguise was terrifying, perhaps more than the reality. This text will step away from any masking, into an examination of the assumptions of life and loss, and will seek to create an applied synthesis of what works, with whom, and under which circumstances, as the reality of death gives way to the survivor's vulnerability and new realities.

II

A Brief History Lesson on Grief and Bereavement in the Western Tradition: Love and Death in a Historic Perspective

"We are imperfect mortal beings, aware of that mortality even as we push it away, failed by our very complication, so wired that when we mourn our losses we also mourn, for better or for worse, ourselves. As we were. As we are no longer. As we will one day not be at all."

Joan Didion, *A Year of Magical Thinking* (2005)

Grief has been a topic of focused scientific and clinical inquiry for a nearly a century. However, in spite of the attention given to such a significant aspect of human existence, progress in gaining a clear understanding of the construct has been relatively slow. This is partially due to the existence of a conceptual problem concerning the definition of grief, making it difficult to identify a single grief response, much less differentiate among multiple grief-related concepts. Clinicians particularly pursuing the practice of grief therapy have had to rely on their individual interpretations of the concept.

To discuss grief and bereavement with clarity, a backdrop is needed, which typically comes from a historical or cultural perspective. Ours begins with the given – that death is a universal experience. However, the response that grief elicits is shaped by the attitudes prevalent in a given culture. Attitudes, including components of belief, emotion, thought, and behavior, develop from the interplay between the individual and the cultural context.

Shared attitudes, often exemplified through language, make a culture distinct since they give nuance and shading to experiences and the meanings ascribed to them. In its pre-modern French origin, the definitions and connotations for grief include the words suffering, distress, wretchedness, pain, burden, and wound. The word also refers to wrongs and injuries that have been inflicted upon an individual by others, which provides the root to the related word *grievance*. There are still other associations, including *greeffe*, *grefe*, and *gravis* – all denoting a heaviness that weighs one down toward the earth, as in gravity, which is the very opposite of levity, or lightness. Grieving people are likely to feel many or all of the emotions inherent in the earliest definitions of the word.

While they may be linguistically erudite, psychological theories and practices are frequently prone neglect the extent to which their subject matter is historically and culturally defined. Regarding death, dying, grief, and bereavement, contemporary orientations have emphasized the importance of breaking the bonds with the deceased and a return of the survivor to an autonomous lifestyle as a universal goal. However, this is a relatively new position.

THE ROMANTIC AGE

Looking back in history to the late 19th century, the romantic ethos of the times said that such breaking of bonds would destroy an individual's identity and the meaning of life. Perhaps as a response to increasing industrialization, this period of time has become known as the "Romantic" era. The term derived from the Romance, a medieval literary form that dealt with events of classical history and legend, such as King Arthur and the Knights of the Round Table (DeSpelder & Strickland, 1999). The Romantic Movement was characterized by a fascination for the supernatural, acts of chivalry, and everlasting loyalty between friends. The romanticists believed in the centrality of the "deep interior" – those mysterious forces and processes, beyond consciousness, that exist somewhere toward the center of one's being and liveliness. Such influences shaped the ideal of "the beautiful death," in which the sad beauty of a loved one's death elicited feelings of melancholy, tinged with optimism for an eventual reunion with the beloved in a heavenly home. Love was eternal and communion with the dead could be maintained through prayer and meditation. Death was not to be hidden from view; it was manageable and part of the ordinary human experience. A death typically occurred at home, and 'home' implied extended generations living together, or at least in close proximity. At the end of life, relatives and friends gathered for a death watch and maintained the vigil at the bedside of the dying person. Following the death, highly personal services were held, often including a wake where the deceased was remembered and memorialized. Burial was the burden of those who had been closest to the deceased in life. From caring for the dying person through final disposal of the corpse, death was held and honored within the realm of the family and close-knit community.

Psychologically, most historical accounts of the theoretical ideas of grief in the Romantic age date to Freud's (1917/1957) *Mourning and Melancholia*. In his writing, Freud changed the rules of grief expression and purpose. He said that the specific function of grief is to detach thoughts and feelings from the deceased so that the bereaved survivor can move on with life. From a psychoanalytic viewpoint, this is seen as an active process, hence, the term grief "work." He wrote,

> Mourning is…"the reaction of the loss of a loved person, or to the loss of some abstraction which has taken the place of one, such as one's country, liberty, an ideal, and so on…It is also well worth notice that, although mourning involves grave departures from the normal attitude of life, it never occurs to us to regard it as a pathological condition and to refer it to medical treatment. We rely on its being overcome after a certain lapse of time, and we look upon any interference with it as useless or even harmful. (1957, pp. 243-244).

In the analytic perspective, the attachment to the deceased must be given up through continued confrontation of memories and thoughts associated with the loss. Freud speculated that pathological grief arises from either avoidance of grief work or conflicting feelings about the deceased. His views challenged the supernatural and spiritual notions of loss and moved the study of grief toward a more scientific, though certainly not an empirically-based view.

During the same time as Freud's musings, a lesser-known theorist named Shand (1920) discussed "the laws of sorrow." His writing concerned individual variations in the grief process, changes over time, the importance of social support, and the additional distress caused by sudden death. He postulated that although expressing thoughts and feelings and disclosing them to others is beneficial, expressing negative emotions causes more intense grief. These notions are prescient for twenty-first century empirical considerations related to grief and bereavement. While Shand's work did not constitute a coherent theory of grief, it did cover a wider range of features than Freud's.

In the 1940s, a researcher named Erich Lindemann identified three primary steps in the progression toward satisfactory coping with loss. Lindemann was an American psychiatrist, specializing in bereavement and noted for his extensive study on the effects of trauma on the survivors and families after the 1942 Coconut Grove fire, a blaze that swept through a Boston nightclub, killing 492 people. As a result of the study, he coined the term 'acute grief', consisting of three steps, including accepting the fact of the loss, adjusting to a life without the deceased, and forming new relationships. Lindemann described grief as a "remarkably uniform" syndrome that includes a common range of physical symptoms such as tightness of throat, shortness of breath, and generalized physical pain, along with a range of emotional responses.

THE MODERNIST AGE

Early in the Romantic era, death was viewed as a part of ordinary human experience. It was incorporated into activities of living. Then later, though still in the early decades of the twentieth century, a significant and sudden change occurred: Once practiced as a public and communal event, death became private (Mellor & Schilling, 1993). The process of dying was progressively hidden from public view and excluded from social life. The deathbed moved from home to hospital. The use of funeral homes became the standard of practice, allowing the rituals of the dead to become more discrete and distant from survivors. Rather than simple wood coffins, elaborate caskets were created, and the deceased was dressed and cleaned to reflect the mortician's cosmetology skills. Typical mortuaries held "slumber rooms" for brief viewings of the embalmed body, no longer impolitely referred to as a corpse. Mourning dress and customary signs identifying the bereaved disappeared. In the proceedings following death, the deceased's family and friends appeared to be onlookers rather than participants, and the tasks of preparing the dead for burial and managing surrounding rituals were professionalized. At the mid-twentieth century, American attitudes for grief became defined as "death denied." By this time, historians had given a new name to the era: The Modernist period.

The chief attributes of the Modernist period were marked by an emphasis on reason, observation, and a faith in continuous progress. Change occurred at a fast pace. Grandmothers would tell their offspring stories of seeing the first automobiles and watching the moon landing during their lifetime. Now, even as their children look on with incredulity, parents recall days before cell phones, microwave ovens, and DVDs. The one assured fact of modern life is that "things change." In the philosophy of the Modernist age, life is approached in a way that emphasizes goal directness, efficiency, and rationality. Metaphorically, the modernist period views life as a well-oiled machine. Everyone has a place and is measured by the success achieved in the performance of whatever task is at hand. Help is redefined by outcome, rather than by care. The notion of service is progressively seen as less important than business productivity. Industry is defined by outcome, rather than by connection. People living from the mid-century forward were enlisted to "do more, do it faster, and do it smarter, with less." Emotionality is seen as an inconvenience and the non-feeling "rugged individualist" becomes the highly favored model of movement through the world. Though the stoic image of the macho police officer, EMT, or fire fighter who "keeps it all in," never showing emotion, has been proven to be physically and psychologically harmful, this remains a highly regarded means of meeting the demands of grief.

At mid-twentieth century, the notion of "death denied" continued to be the model of choice. In 1959, Herman Feifel brought together a group of multidisciplinary authorities whose theoretical, cultural, and clinical essays formed the book *The Meaning of Death*. The conclave and its resulting work were formative, especially considering the prevailing resistance to discussing death. Feifel wrote,

> The realization soon began to sink in that what I was up against were not idiosyncratic personal quirks, the usual administrative vicissitudes, pique, or non-acceptance of an inadequate research design. Rather, it was a personal position, bolstered by cultural structuring, that death is a dark symbol not to be stirred – not even touched – an obscenity to be avoided. (1990/1963, p. 25)

Feifel recalled that he was told by a learned colleague that to be truly empathic, "the only thing you never do is to discuss death with a patient." In counterpoint, literary works such as C.S. Lewis' *A Grief Observed* began to bring grief and bereavement issues to greater prominence (though Lewis was strongly sanctioned by his peers for talking openly and publicly about his feelings regarding the death of his wife, Joy Lewis).

As a benchmark of this late middle period of the twentieth century, a new rubric of death awareness was proposed. The hypothesis commonly known as the 'five stages of grief' was introduced by psychiatrist Elisabeth Kübler-Ross in the late 1960s. The Kübler-Ross model, from her book *On Death and Dying (1969)*, was inspired by her work with terminally ill patients. This stage theory emerged from Kübler-Ross's distress concerning the lack of death and dying curricula in medical schools. With a select group of peers and patients at the University of Chicago medical school where she taught, Kübler-Ross initiated a qualitative research project about the process of death and the "death denied" silence surrounding it. The results were fascinating and evolved into a series of professional and public seminars. Those interviews, along with her research, led to one of the seminal and best-selling texts of the twentieth century, even though the body of her work was never validated with any scientific rigor. It remains unclear how her data were collected and analyzed. Even with its poor methodology, her work had monumental social significance and revolutionized how medical and social science professionals take care of the terminally ill. As a result of its publication, a demand was created for a new way to approach dying patients. The book, still popular in the lay literature, calls for more humanistic care and offers a more affirming message than had been previously discussed, i.e., talking to a dying person about the experience of the process has value and meaning. Kübler-Ross's research was quickly co-opted into the social experience of the Modernist era and molded to fit exquisitely with the zeitgeist of the times. Care for the terminally ill quickly and erroneously became applied to grief following death. Her stage theory gave a productive purpose to grief. As the bereaved individual achieved the benchmarks described by the stage, the survivor moved one step closer to the productive ideal of acceptance.

Dr. Kübler-Ross' later writings held that these stages are not meant to be complete or chronological, even though the book and subsequent writings give the clear impression of linear stages that an individual proceeds through in a step-wise manner. In her later writings, the theory states that not everyone who experiences a life-threatening or life-altering event feels all five of the responses, nor will those who do experience them move in any particular order. Rather, the hypothesis holds that the reactions to illness, death, and loss are as unique as the person experiencing them. Even though her work was not empirically validated, her five stages of grief became widely accepted through the remainder of the twentieth century. In later iterations, primary criticism was raised at the tendency to prescribe rather than describe grief. It is unclear whether the stages represent a description of how persons cope with dying or as a prescriptive approach that stresses individuals ought to be assisted to move through the five stages, eventually embracing acceptance.

Because the hypothesis is so well-known though, bereaved people tend to rush or get pressured to move sequentially through the stages, instead of letting them happen naturally (if at all). There is some kind of "imaginary" schedule connected to the stages, which is incorrectly thought to be met in a linear, goal-directed fashion.

Much of Kübler-Ross' work focuses on the notion of denial. Denial and its correlate – acceptance – are much more complex than perceived. In the 1970s, a psychiatrist named Weisman studied the superficiality of Kübler-Ross's use of the terms and their functions. He described different behavioral manifestations attributed to denial, such as discounting symptoms, diagnosis, or impending death. Weisman (1972) noted denial to be a fully-functional defense mechanism, and as such, serves a protective function for the psyche. Denial allows individuals to participate in treatment, therapy, and to sustain hope. To amplify his description of the process, Weisman introduced the concept of 'middle knowledge', defined as the time that patients drift in and out of denial, sometimes affirming and other times distancing from the closeness of death.

ATTACHMENT

Around the same time of Kübler-Ross' original work, the nature of attachments to others and the process by which those attachments are relinquished following a loss were discussed as central concerns in the work of John Bowlby, one of the more influential theorists writing about the nature of grief. Bowlby believed that human emotional bonds "arise out of deep seated, innate mechanisms which have evolved in order to ensure survival" (Parkes, Laungani & Young 1997, p. 246). He argued that babies have innate physical features and behaviors that elicit care and protection from older group members. Bowlby speculated that infants possess a motivational "attachment system designed by natural selection to regulate and maintain proximity between infants and their caregivers" (Fraley and Shaver, 1999, p. 736). The theory implies that a cause-effect relationship exists between early attachment patterns and later reactions to bereavement, and makes the argument that "whether an individual exhibits a healthy or problematic pattern of grief following separation depends on the way his or her attachment system has become organized over the course of development" (Fraley and Shaver, 1999, p. 740).

According to attachment theory, when a bereaved individual perceives that the loved object no longer exists, grief springs forth, along with a defensive demand to withdraw libidinal energy from the object to which it had been attached. The demand meets with psychic opposition, causing the survivor to temporarily turn away from reality in an attempt to cling to the lost object. By repeatedly engaging in the work of grieving, i.e., realistically turning toward the loss, the libido, defined as life-giving psychological energy, eventually becomes detached from the love object, and the ego becomes free of its clinging attachment to the deceased (Bowlby, 1969). Bowlby shed new light on humans' deep emotional bonds with attachment figures and their powerful emotional reactions to separation and loss: disbelief, horror, angry protest, and despair. These reactions have now been studied and validated in empirical detail by developmental psychologists.

As noted, one of the core tenets of attachment theory is that humans are born with an innate psychobiological system motivating the infant to seek proximity to significant others in times of need and as protection from threat and distress (Bowlby, 1969). Primarily during childhood, the individual comes to know and progressively attaches to primary figures that serve to soothe and comfort in times of vulnerability. Bowlby thought the attachment system was most important early in life, though he acknowledged its activity over the entire life span (Bowlby, 1988). He postulated that people of all ages are capable of forming attachment bonds with stronger and wiser others. Therefore, they feel distress on separation or loss of these persons. Bonds occur with a variety of close attachment figures, including siblings, friends, and romantic partners. The attachment behavioral system is activated by perceived threats and dangers, which cause a frightened individual to seek proximity with protective others. Attaining proximity and protection result in feelings of relief and a sense of security. Satisfying the attachment need makes it possible to explore the world with curiosity and confidence and to engage in rewarding interactions with other people. Bowlby viewed this sense of attachment security as crucial for maintaining emotional stability, developing a solid and authentic sense of self-worth, and forming mutually satisfying, long-lasting close relationships.

According to attachment theory, the loss of an attachment figure is a devastating event that triggers intense and pervasive distress. Initially, the survivor cannot imagine regaining a sense of security, support, protection, and love without this person's availability and responsiveness. Through a series of reactions to the loss, the bereaved individual moves through phases related to the separation, eventually giving way to detachment, marked by an apparent recovery and gradual renewal of interest in other activities and new relationship partners. In his later writing, Bowlby preferred to call the final phase of separation distress 'reorganization' rather than 'detachment' because of its transfer of proximity seeking and search for a safe haven and secure base. According to the theory, adults do not need to defensively detach from a lost attachment figure and suppress all feelings, thoughts, or memories of the deceased. Instead, Bowlby believes the survivor can rearrange representations of self and the deceased, so that the relationship continues to serve as a symbolic source of protection, comfort, and love while life with others continues on new foundations.

Around the same time as Bowlby and Kübler-Ross were studying, Cicely Saunders wrote a pioneering work, *Care of the Dying* (1967), which sparked interest in hospice care. Saunders emphasized that dying was not simply a biomedical or physical event, but also has psychosocial, familial, and spiritual implications. Therefore, care of the dying needed to be holistic and centered on the intimate system at the end of life. The concept of hospice is to create a "home-like" atmosphere and a comprehensive, embracing way to allow dying people to live their remaining days as fully as possible, free from debilitating pain and incapacitating symptoms. In the last quarter of the 20th century, the holistic philosophy of hospice permeated much of medicine, at least in terms of the recognition that a patient's quality of life means meeting not only physical needs but psychological, social, and spiritual needs as well. The growth of hospice allowed for medicine to consider healing in addition to curative processes, and questioned the medical ethic of heroic interventions at end-of-life.

In the early 1980s, William Worden published *Grief Counseling and Grief Therapy* (1982), bringing a paradigm shift to the stage theory so fully embraced two decades earlier. Worden conceptualizes grief and mourning as a series of four tasks, with an assumption of individuality and autonomy not seen in the stage models. In his theory, grieving individuals move through these tasks on a personal timetable, without any assumption of linearity. Some might skip tasks, others might linger on those found to be more difficult and troublesome. Worden's work is noted as one of the earliest to speak to the nature of adaptation to loss, which would be studied with greater scientific rigor in the next century.

GRIEF UNDERSTOOD IN THE TWENTY-FIRST CENTURY

Contemporary research on grief and bereavement continues to be more theory driven than qualitatively applied. Many researchers explain the theoretical approach as necessary to understand the oftentimes counter-intuitive phenomena and complex symptomatology of grief. From a philosophical point of view, theories explain individual differences in response to loss and guide the development of care and intervention strategies that alleviate distress and prevent complications.

Early in the twenty-first century, a call came from the professional community to develop an integrative theory of grief and bereavement. To date, this call goes unanswered. Instead, there are multiple, valid theoretical approaches to grief, with a variety of paradigms and rubrics directed to understanding symptomatology and coping at both the general and grief-specific levels. As one researcher notes, "...there is still no comprehensive evidence-based theory to account for the way in which people move from initial high levels of distress to levels similar to those before the loss" (Archer, 2008, p. 58). However, there are good theories that link grief to the nature of the relationship that was lost, to the relationship's meaning for the survivor, and to the ways that the relationship may have served regulatory functions for the living. There is also a fair amount of study reifying grief as profoundly shaped by the family context in which it occurs.

What seems to be most figural in the contemporary understanding of grief is the movement away from the medical perspective of grief-as-bereavement and grief as a pathological experience from which the survivor must recover. Contemporary views of grief focus on multiple aspects of the experience. There is a consensus that emotional states differ considerably among bereaved people and that the temporal course of grief may reflect diverse trajectories, rather than stages or phases, both before and after the death of a loved one. However, although bereaved individuals show great variation in the sequencing and experience of affective states, there is also validity to the idea of a general and predictable progression of grief states. Acknowledging this makes it easier to think about the changes as the expression of grieving as time passes.

Interesting research is emerging: In addition to assessing problematic outcomes of grief, examination of more positive outcomes has begun to hold scholarly value. Traditionally, intrapersonal approaches to understanding grief and adaptation have been the focus of time and attention. This stance is becoming more balanced by interpersonal orientations, particularly in relationship to coping. The positive psychology movement has gained traction in the last decade, and its application to the experience of grief and bereavement has revealed the need to integrate positive mental and physical health outcomes, including improved self-efficacy and psychological well-being in the presence and integration of loss. The larger body of the contemporary grief literature says that focus should move away from 'one size fits all' and "...just move to a science in which not everyone can be measured on everything, in which measurement is always a matter of great skepticism, in which contradiction and difference count for a lot" (Rosenblatt, 2008, p. 243).

The early Modernist approaches continue to influence understandings of acute grief, though more contemporary models emphasize grief as a natural response to major transitions in life. Bonds between the grieving individual and the lost object continue, albeit in different forms, after the loss. Approaches that date to the 1990s began to emphasize a significant loss as shattering personal assumptions, causing grieving individuals to reconstruct a redefined sense of self, spirituality, and relationship to others and the world. While this is a painful process, it may also be a catalyst for growth. In the last two decades, those reading the grief research literature saw new terms associated with the construct, including posttraumatic growth, meaning-making, and meaning reconstruction. The body of research related to growth-as-a-result-of-grief remains complex and tangled, since there are many differing components included in the term "growth" and "meaning." Depending on what the research trajectory holds, there are distinctions among perceived benefits, sustained growth, or insight, among many different outcomes discussed and measured.

Grief researchers are building theoretical models to foster integration of these complex, interacting variables that determine individual differences in adaptation. These models are in early stages of development and will require a good deal of examination before they are accepted and applied as best practice. Many researchers are making the case for investigating multiple factors in one design, concurrently studying constructs such as the qualities of resilience, long-term adaptation to early loss, or secondary loss and its relation to psychological risk and vulnerability. At the same time, there are just as many researchers who continue to study and analyze single factors, such as dimensions of religion and its relevance to grief.

Contemporary grief research is requiring an accounting for the impact of societal changes and the interpersonal phenomena related to information technology. Grieving is seen as a significant interaction among individual experiences, circumstances, and social forces. Because of such changes, it is likely that new manifestations of grief may emerge. Examples abound: People in Western societies are now more accepting of the significance of a partner in an unmarried cohabitating couple, whether it be heterosexual or homosexual. Death following prolonged illness, coupled with advances in medicine, changes the nature and understanding of suffering and of heroic efforts. The old adage "we want everything done that can be done" has new meaning, since the lines between life and death become quite blurry when considering highly technical medical interventions.

The sense of cultural continuity has begun to change. Anthropologists know that cohesion among generations and ethnic boundaries are vulnerable to sociological and technological shifts. For generations, 'place' has been a connector between generations and marked the passages of youth into adulthood and old age. Now, for society in general, place has given way to flux. The notion of 'home' is not where most people were born, died, and where the family shared and addressed their systemic concerns. The world is smaller and people are mobile and fluid in their life experience. Home is where you 'hang your hat' at the moment. There is less of a sense of being settled in one place, whether between generations, communities, or professions. While rural areas have maintained tradition longer, even in remote and frontier areas everything moves faster and the big has become bigger.

The lack of continuity gives rise to new social connotations regarding loss and disenfranchisement, pointing toward a pronounced need to assess how grief reactions vary in intensity, process, and outcome related to the complexities caused by social networking, on-line grief support, and the speed of information offered by the World Wide Web. There is a sense, too, that people know each other through the pseudo-intimacy connecting them in the technological world. When a death occurs, the private sense of loss may be eroded by an undemanding image of connection and a sense of pseudo community, one that increasingly replaces face-to-face relationships with the nuclear and extended family, church, and neighborhood. The confusion deepens as the prevailing model of grief and bereavement emphasizes separateness and puts a positive value on autonomy and individuation while devaluing interdependence. Such a cultural shift begs the questions asked by grief researcher Robert Kastenbaum when he writes,

> "How meaningful is a death that does not occur within an established pattern of meaning? And what if death itself becomes the pattern? What if the transition from life to death should lose its impact of immediacy and instead become another cork floating in a confused sea of mediated experiences?" (2008, p. 68)

In recent years, there has been an expansion of research evaluating the efficacy of psychological interventions for grief and bereavement distress. Applied challenges continue to require focus and attention. It is now recognized that grief is more than sorrow and emotional turmoil. Five dimensions of grief are receiving particular attention in the mental health community. First, stress reactions, including changes in physiological function that can increase one's vulnerability to illness and exacerbate preexisting physical problems are being applied to loss. Second, perception and thought are affected by loss, with the increased possibility of making impulsive and potentially harmful decisions and manifesting more risk for accidents. Third, a spiritual crisis often occurs, where the guiding assumptions and values are called into question. Fourth, family and communal response to loss, often neglected in the past, is a significant factor in grief and grief recovery. Finally, although the pain of loss may be universal, cultural heritage and current support systems have great influence on the expression of loss coping styles in the presence of stress. Grief therapy seems least effective when offered in general ways, irrespective of indications that interventions are needed. It seems to be more effective for those people who are empirically regarded as vulnerable, and as most effective for those who have complicated grief, grief-related depression, or posttraumatic disorders.

In perspective, contemporary approaches do not see bereavement or grieving as ever fully resolved, culminating in 'closure' or 'recovery'. Rather than emphasizing letting go, a negotiation process unfolds to understand and incorporate the meaning of the loss over time. While the death is permanent and unchanging, the process is not. Grief therapy, at this point in time, generally operates from the assumption that while mourning practices may vary, grief remains grief. It cannot change in a significant way because it is intrinsic to the human condition.

III

The Experience of Loss

"Where you used to be, there is a hole in the world, which I find myself constantly walking around in the daytime, and falling in at night. I miss you like hell."

Edna St. Vincent Millay

Throughout time, humanity has been concerned with mortality and loss. In the twenty-first century, technological advances continue to be employed in an attempt to understand and control death. In spite of these leaps, the reality remains: Death is inevitable, and this knowledge determines how much of life is viewed.

PHILOSOPHICALLY SPEAKING

Twenty-first century philosophers speak to the tradition of death as figural in the understanding of life. In existential thought, death is not viewed negatively, but holds the awareness of mortality as one of the basic human conditions giving significance to living. Life, as it is known, is inconceivable without the tacit assumption that it must end. Without an appreciation of death, such things as reproduction, emotion, competition, and ambition would be pointless. This distinguishing human characteristic is contained in the ability to grasp realities of the future, the inevitability of death, and the fact of human finiteness with limited time, all of which make life more poignant and meaningful. Existentialists believe it to be necessary to think about death in order to consider the significance of life. From this philosophical viewpoint, death is not considered a threat. Instead, it provides motivation to take advantage of appreciating the present moment. Although the notion

19

of death serves as a continuing wake-up call to life, it is something that most people in western society avoid, primarily because it elicits anxiety. Anxiety arises from the recognition of the realities of mortality, the confrontation of pain and suffering, the human need to struggle for survival, and the realization of personal vulnerability and fallibility. When in the presence of the anxieties associated with death, grief arises. Grief is the natural process of psychological, social, and somatic reactions to the perception of loss.

The confrontation with death and loss is a significant element of being human. In spite of individuality and uniqueness, all will die. As the writer John Morgan says, "We, and every one we love, will die. In spite of our uniqueness, we are still radically contingent and will someday cease to be" (1993, p. 5). As has been duly noted, to live in the world requires continuing confrontation with issues of loss. Loss, then, is a part of everyday existence, and always results in deprivation of some kind. While many losses are clearly perceived as unpleasant deprivations, e.g., the death of a spouse, other losses are the result of ordinary development and change, such as the birth of a child, which brings the loss of a relative amount of independence. It is simply in the nature of loss to grieve. Grief, in response to loss, is the process that allows the individual to incorporate "that which was" and make room for "that which is to come." In the contextual loss of grief following a literal death, the process encourages readjustment to the external where the deceased is no longer present, and then to incorporate internal memories helping the survivor reorganize and recover a new sense of balance.

There are multiple pragmatic descriptions of the grief process, beginning with Freud and moving through contemporary theorists. Several of these models have been described in Chapter Two. There is wide opinion that regards the work of Parkes and Weiss (1983) as holding a cogent and relevant paradigm to examine in grief therapy. They write that three tasks must be accomplished in order for recovery from grief to take place:

1. **Intellectual recognition and explanation of the loss**. The bereaved individual develops an explanation of how the loss happened that answers all questions, ultimately identifying an inevitable cause of the death. Without such an explanation, the one who is grieving cannot relax the vigilance against the threat of new loss and will therefore continue to feel anxious.

2. **Emotional acceptance of the loss.** The survivor reaches a point where reminders of the loss are no longer too painful to face. This state of mind

happens after repeated confrontations with every element of the loss, through obsessive review of thoughts, memories, and feelings, and with gradual changes in emphasis and focus. Such a review may be avoided early in grief, not as true denial, but as a form of distancing to gain respite from the pain. The obsessive review and denial only become problems when they are continued too long, with "too long" being defined by distress and disability.

3. **Assumption of a new identity.** The survivor gradually develops a new identity that reflects new circumstances of life. The process begins as the griever becomes uncomfortably aware of the discrepancy between the world that is now and the world that was.

Movement toward this new identity is slow and halting, and there may be times when the survivor "forgets" the new status or acts as if the deceased is still present. According to these theorists, the speed of the progress to integrate the loss is not important as long as progress is being made.

THE DETERMINATION OF DEATH

Even though it seems to be a redundant exercise, it is necessary to define death. In any dictionary, death is the biological event that occurs naturally to all living things. It is the absence of life and a passage from this existence into the next. A simple definition of death is "the transition from the state of being alive to the state of being dead" (Kass, 1971, p. 699). While an elegant definition, it does not help with the broader, more philosophical understandings associated with the meaning of death. This conundrum is complicated by advances in medicine and increased research knowledge which muddy rather than clarify the question "When is a person dead?" As one writer asked, "Is it at that point when all the cells of the body have ceased to function (biological death) or when heart and lung function can no longer be detected (cardiac death) or when the person is said to be in a persistent vegetative state (psychological death)?" (Meagher, 2007, p. 173)

There are several definitions of death. By the early 1980s, as medical technology was making quantum leaps, the Harvard Ad Hoc Committee on Brain Death Syndrome provided four criteria for determining death: Unreceptivity and unresponsivity, no detectable movement or breathing, no reflect response, and a flat EEG. Around the same time, a presidential commission proposed that the determination of death be made in accordance with accepted medical standards, defined by the judgment that an individual has sustained either an irreversible cessation of circulatory and respiratory functions, or an irreversible cessation of all functions of the entire brain, including the brain stem. This definition was included in the Uniform Determination of Death Act (1981). The criteria in the act are based on the certainty that loss of function in the systems is independent of the use of any life-sustaining technology. The declaration does not mean that there are no bodily processes taking place. It does mean that if any organ or system is functioning, current technologies are not sensitive enough to detect it.

Brain death is a clinical diagnosis that can be made when a decision has been reached that there is complete and irreversible cessation of all brain function. Since it is now possible to sustain cardiac, circulatory, respiratory, and other organ function after the brain has ceased to be alive, a diagnosis of brain death criteria can be made before the heart beat stops (Phillips, 2005).

"Learning to Surf:" A Case Study

A lovely middle-aged woman told the story of her mother's death several years prior. "She was in her mid-80s, and in relatively good health. She lived alone, had an active social life, good friends, and didn't need a great deal of care. Then Daddy died in the autumn and Mother began a slow decline. She just lost her spark for life. I felt like she had just folded up her tent. My brother and I began to make more frequent visits, until I found myself going to see her every day. I worried about her more and was monitoring her life much more closely. She was doing all right for several months until she fell and broke her hip. It was a rapid decline from there.

"When she first got to the hospital, it turned out she had a small stroke, and then had several more in the next few days. It was like she lost her physical health and her mind all at the same time. After a few days, the doctors told me that she was brain dead, even though her physical body still kept working. It was pneumonia that finally took her, thank goodness. Mother hadn't told any of us her wishes for how she wanted to be cared for, about anything related to a funeral, or the disposition of her estate. We should've known better since Daddy's death had been so recent, but it was just easier not to deal with it.

"I look back on that time and feel like I was swimming in the ocean. Nothing seemed normal; there was no ground to stand on. My emotions came and went with the tides. I was sad beyond words. There were days that I felt an emotional undertow I thought would drown me. Other days I felt relief. Then I felt guilty for feeling relieved. And that made me sad, all over again. A friend asked me how I was dealing with the struggle and I told her about my image of being in the ocean. She said, 'Well, I guess you can't control the waves, so I hope you learn to surf.' I know she was trying to be clever. She didn't realize how wise her words were, and I took them to heart. That one statement helped me learn how to manage my grief, and I am forever grateful for this."

GRIEF THAT COMES IN WAVES

Researchers have begun to actively theorize about what clinicians have observed for years. The metaphor the woman provided is an accurate description of grief: There is a wavelike nature to the process. Robert Kastenbaum, one of the first social scientists to write about adaptation to death and loss, wrote, "Distress does not end with the first wave of shock and grief. After the realization that a loved one is dead often comes the realization that life is supposed to go on" (1977, p. 138). One particularly thoughtful theory amplifies Kastenbaum's thoughts; it is called the 'dual process model' of coping with bereavement. It proposes that, to effectively meet the demands of loss, an oscillation between two separate processes must occur (Stroebe & Schut, 1999). The two processes, which come in waves, move between loss and restoration. The "loss-oriented" wave involves focusing on some aspect of the loss experience itself, most particularly with respect to the deceased person. The corresponding wave is "restoration-oriented." In this wave, there is movement beyond the loss to focus on the tasks and demands of life without the deceased and on what needs to be done to restore typical functioning. The theory reiterates the common theme similar to most contemporary thought, that grieving is not static but involves a regular tidal flow between loss and restoration.

Emotionality goes hand in hand with grief and loss. In the example above, the woman describes a loss of "normality" as she entered into the demands of care giving, then after her mother's death, experiencing the enormity of the loss. Such changes in ordinary daily rhythms, accompanied by additional new and unexplored feelings, can cause distress and disorientation. The unfolding grief is highly personal and idiosyncratic. What fits for one may be dreadful for another. In grief, "normality," which is generally employed as a social barometer, as one person said, "…to figure out if I'm acting the way that I should be" – is lost.

For everyone, emotions build and peak like waves. During typical times of life, management of affect is predictable and familiar. On a routine basis, individuals are exposed to a wide variety of experiences called "arousing stimuli" by psychologists. The word 'emotion' is used to describe this arousal. In Latin, emotion means "to move" and in the Old French, "to excite." Scientifically speaking, emotions are complicated collections of chemical and neural responses that respond to relations among external events, thoughts, and changes in internal feeling states. Emotions are noticed and named as affects, also known as feelings, and unfold in the mind. Until a person notices the arousal, no thought occurs about what is happening or what should happen. Even when the arousal goes unnoticed, the emotion continues to drive the behavior (which speaks to the psychodynamic notion of unconscious process). Emotions are felt by the body (though not necessarily in the conscious mind) and displayed to others. The subjective aspect of emotion is called a 'felt sense,' and corresponds to how the individual responds or not to the arousal. Implicit in the discussion of feelings is the defining notion that includes sensory and tactile experiences as well as a range of emotional and affective responses, both pleasurable and painful.

Emotional regulation is the term psychologists use to define the proper ability to manage emotions in the presence of such sensory arousal. Simply put, this is the degree that an individual is able to be in affective control. Emotional regulation involves a complex process of initiating, inhibiting, or modulating the four aspects of functioning. The first aspect involves an internal feeling state, which is the subjective experience of the emotion. The body sends the message "Pay attention, something is happening." Once felt, thoughts correspond to the feeling. The mind says, "Let's get motivated and decide how to respond." The third aspect then involves physiological processes associated with the feeling, including such things as change of heart rate, blood pressure, and hormonal shifts. The psychic question becomes figural: "Am I going to fight what is threatening me, run and hide from it, or am I just frozen and stuck in it?" Finally, there are actions related to the emotion, with hopes that the individual has a sufficient repertoire of experience to choose a wise and prudent course of action. The goal of emotional regulation is to help an individual maintain attention to tasks and express or suppress behavior in response to the stimulus under consideration. Under ordinary circumstances, most people are sufficiently flexible in their emotional processing to manage effectively, even in the presence of more extreme emotional states. Such fluid movement allows for contentment and satisfaction, most of the time.

However, grief is a strange phenomenon. Even with common threads defining its process, it is highly personal with many actions whirring in concurrent motion in its presence. Such movement makes it difficult to gain a feel for an experience, particularly when the meaning of the world is transformed in ways outside of comprehension. In the mind's eye, grief following loss can be imagined as waves crashing in at the shoreline – powerful, irresistible, unpredictable, and with rhythmic highs and lows. For a while, grief leaves the survivor feeling undeniably out of control of nearly everything associated with the loss. Survivors feel they have few choices and options.

Such a state of being causes many grief and bereavement scholars to write about "negative feelings." This is a fundamental error. There are no negative feelings – they are what they are. Granted, some emotions bring pain, others frustration, and still others distress. However, it is in the nature of feeling states to activate an individual's attention. Grief brings emotional dysregulation, which is oftentimes more alarming than necessary.

In the grief experience, there are common emotional states worthy of exploration, particularly in terms of their functionality and purpose in the presence of grief and loss. They are sadness, anger, guilt, hope, anxiety, and love.

Sadness

One of the key components of grief is intense sadness. In the face of grief, sadness is more than an abstract concept. In the presence of a profound loss, sadness penetrates the source of a person's being and can be all-encompassing and bottomless. The emotion of sadness emerges when a loss occurs and there is nothing, nothing, nothing that can be done about it. In its purest form, sadness is essentially about resignation. Characteristically, when an individual feels sad, there is a lowering of mood accompanied by feelings of disadvantage, despair, helplessness, sorrow, and rage.

Sadness has great value and utility in grief recovery. It turns attention inward, allowing the individual to take stock and adjust (Sterns, 1993). It has been said that with sadness comes accuracy. The survivor becomes more detail-oriented and is likely to make fewer memory errors (Bonanno, 2009). However, there is also a tendency to become ruminative, which may become troublesome over time if thoughts and memories begin to "spin" rather than change. Generally, sadness has been seen as something to "shake off." There is import in the capacity to allow sadness to dwell in the psyche, since the feeling is a natural and an expected response to loss. Staying with sadness requires a fair amount of emotional support from self and others. The capacity to wholeheartedly be sad, without pushing the experience away, is essential to allow grief 'breathing room' and engagement.

Toleration of sadness, in the presence of grief, is a significant sign of psychological health. Beginning in infancy, an individual experiences sensations of distress that accompany an unmet need. This is the first experience of frustration. Sadness accompanies the sensation and the infant learns to put a moment between impulse and action. The same process is employed later in life for those who grieve. During bereavement, the function of sadness becomes an essential tool for facilitating acceptance and accommodation to the loss. The loss and its corresponding sadness bring the individual into the presence of what is missing and how personal needs are left unmet. Sadness is a slow emotion and makes the world sluggish. As one fellow said, "After my wife died, living with the sadness was like living in slow motion." Over time, through revisiting every aspect of the loss, the survivor makes reappraisals of the deceased, which ultimately lessens the psychological impact. The intensity of sadness lifts as memories of the deceased are incorporated into the survivor's lived experience.

The fellow above continued, saying, "I could not control it, and after a while, that was OK. I guess I didn't need to pay as much attention to the world around me. I just put aside everything that I would normally do, including most of my everyday concerns, and turned my attention inward. There were plenty of times that I felt lost, and that's when I had a couple of good friends who could pull me out of it."

Sadness can become troublesome when the griever becomes overwhelmed by reflection. When this happens, preoccupation with the loss becomes so figural that immediate needs and responsibilities, or the needs of intimates, are marginalized. Fortunately, sadness comes equipped with a built-in safety mechanism. People who feel sad, look sad, especially during bereavement (Bonanno & Keltner, 1997). Whether aware of it or not, such body language signals to others the need for help. Sad expressions are very effective in eliciting sympathy, understanding, and the help of other people. This is an optimistic sign for the offering of empathy, compassion, and concern for those in the presence of the sadness of grief.

ANGER

Along with joy, surprise, fear, disgust, and sadness, anger is known as a primary human emotion (Campos et al., 1939). It is psychologically interpreted as having been offended, overpowered, wronged, or denied, and involves a tendency to react through retaliation. It is the perception that something has gone wrong and needs to be attended to. Anger is felt when a person makes the conscious choice to take action to stop whatever feels threatening. It seeks an outlet for expression.

While some people are temperamentally and constantly angry, in grief, anger seems to be more episodic. It manifests as a way of mobilizing personal and psychological resources and boosts the sense of personal determination to correct a wrongdoing, in this case – death. All emotions vary in intensity; anger is no different. In its stronger form, anger impairs the ability to process the information necessary to allow the individual to exert cognitive control over behavior. As anger escalates, there are corresponding losses of objectivity, empathy, caution, and thoughtfulness. There are sharp distinctions between anger and aggression, even though they mutually influence each other. While anger can activate aggression or increase its probability or intensity, it is neither a necessary nor a sufficient condition for aggressive behavior.

Anger is misunderstood in Western society. At its most essential, anger helps the griever to individuate. In its more positive light, it is used to protect the self in physical, emotional, intellectual, and spiritual dimensions of relationships. When a death has occurred, the grieving survivor's vulnerability and frailty demands the sense of self-protection that anger can provide. The protection and separation processes of anger frame the emotion much more favorably than rage. Anger, as an emotion, can separate and protect, much more capably than rage.

Rage is construed as an attempt to summon help for survival in the experience of terror and threat. Rage is an overwhelming experience and can be conceptualized as an inability to process emotions or life experiences. As one fellow said as he described his experience of rage, "It was just a whole lot of different feelings trying to get out all at once." Such raw, undifferentiated emotions that spill out when a life event cannot be processed, putting too much stress on the organism.

Anger holds heat and rage is a similarly hot emotion. But, anger is guided by thought. People feel angry when they sense an offense, are certain that someone is responsible for the insult, and that there is some influence that can be brought to bear to cope with or change the situation. Usually, those who experience anger explain its arousal as a result of "what happened to me." In most cases, anger presents as a response to a provocation coming from a discrete, external cause. The angry person usually finds the cause of anger in an intentional, personal, and controllable aspect of another's behavior. In grief, there is often no single external precipitant. Its origin is multi-causal, with the anger emerging from the sense of helplessness associated with the absolute finiteness of death and the losses brought by the absence of the deceased.

Anger is a complicated emotion. It makes people think more optimistically, though increases the likelihood of making risky decisions. It makes a person less trusting and slower to attribute good qualities to those perceived as "outsiders." An angry person tends to anticipate, focusing attention on the loss and any other wrongs that may be related to the death. It leads the bereaved to feel more desire for the object of the anger is tied. Anger alerts an individual to the loss of the possession of the relationship, and motivates continued confrontation of the loss.

GUILT

Guilt is an emotional warning sign that most people learn through predictable childhood development. It is defined as moral reasoning. The origin of the word comes from the old English word that variously means crime, sin, fault, fine, or debt. In many definitions it is synonymous with regret. Guilt alerts an individual to the sense of wrong doing, encouraging the development of a better sense of behavior. The focus of guilt is on self-actions and behaviors that can be undertaken to repair a failure. It works as a prompt for re-examining behavior in order to keep from repeating mistakes. It creates an affective state of conflict following the perception of a mistake or misjudgment, is driven by conscience, and is most often accompanied by anxiety.

The conscience is that piece of personality holding the capacity to rationally weigh principles of responsibility. Literally, it is the ability to respond. The conscience, which houses guilt, contains all of the external standards set by parental authorities, in family and society, and is practiced from childhood through adult life. It guides good behavior and establishes prohibitions against unrestrained desires and wishes that could hurt others. The conscience holds images of authority, which becomes constant and consistent parts of the personality. It is the Jiminy Cricket of the mind.

In relation to grief, guilt quickly becomes antagonistic and is driven by a tyranny of shoulds. The 'shoulds' of life reflect an idealized image of the self, defined by a rigid, unrealistic picture of what one ought to be. From infancy and early childhood, individuals are taught to maintain personal rules that underlie many of the things that 'should' be done. They are practiced because of a social desire to be liked and accepted by other people. Individuals take on many of the community's rules, which become part of the belief system of "how (I) should be." Under ordinary circumstances, 'shoulds' function like the accelerator and brake of a car, governing the speed between thought and action. In the presence of grief, the shoulds can cause trouble, since prevailing social rules may not fit well with the personal belief system. To push the metaphor, the mechanics of the car change and act in unexpected ways. Most times the 'shoulds' do not activate on a conscious level until there is a stimulus that causes the person to think of them. Whenever the bereaved tries to behave according to the belief that "things must be a certain way," emotional pressure increases, leading to upsets and loss of balance. Grief, in its idiosyncratic manifestation, rarely fits social rules and regulations, but takes a course of its own, leaving the survivor feeling guilty for not behaving in socially normative or idealized ways.

Guilt is like sadness, since both bring specific focus to an object, event, or circumstance for evaluation. For the bereaved grieving the death of a significant other, this powerful emotional system erroneously signals that something "should" have been done in some socially expected way. Guilt points an individual toward some corrective action. When a person cannot help another, or fails in efforts to do so, the experience of guilt lurks nearby. For better or worse, most survivors, while examining and re-examining the relationship with the deceased, find memories of ruptures, mistakes, and regrets of things undone. There are multiple social, emotional, and psychological missteps to be considered in any life well lived, leaving survivors at odds with themselves and the deceased. Most people have difficulty dealing with the emotional ambivalence of "things that should have been." Also, most people have particular difficulty in dealing with feelings of anger. Since guilt is defined by something "wrong," feeling angry, resentful, or hostile about the deceased, or about the way grief unravels social expectations, is experienced as unacceptable and gives rise to the unpleasant experience.

Guilt is discouraged in contemporary society. However, there is healthy guilt. In bereavement, guilt works best to help the survivor grow and mature by allowing close examination of "the good, the bad, and the ugly" in the historical relationship with the deceased. The presence of guilt signals the need to consider a behavior change. It is left to the bereaved to determine the most appropriate course of action. Guilt serves the purpose to offer an opportunity for redirecting moral or behavioral compasses. Everyone feels guilt, but to different degrees and about different things. This is all dependent on what a person believes about what is right and what is wrong.

HOPE

An old Arab proverb says, "when you have hope, you have everything." Hope is first seen in the Greek mythological story of Zeus and Prometheus. Prometheus stole fire from the god Zeus, infuriating the supreme god. In retaliation and punishment, Zeus created a box that contained all manner of evil, unknown to and hidden from the receiver of the box. The box was eventually given to Pandora, who opened it even after being warned away. The evils were released into the world. Hope, which lay at the bottom of the box, remained. Thus began the tale of Hope. In contemporary thought, hope is any possibility greater than zero that an objective can be reached. More formally, it is the emotional state promoting the belief in a positive outcome related to personal events and circumstances. It sits at the other end of the continuum from despair. Hope looks forward, with desire and reasonable confidence for something favorable to happen. It is an enduring state.

As an individual grieves, hope tiptoes in, quietly and gently neutralizing despair. The word 'resolve' comes to mind when considering hope. Rather than serving as a synonym for acceptance or repair, to re-solve a problem or state of being allows it to be seen in a different light. This is the structure of hope. Earlier discussions explored sadness as the emotion that focuses attention. In turn, hope opens and broadens the individual's sight and removes the blinders of fear and despair, allowing the perspective for a new, bigger picture to emerge. It brings the bereaved into the presence of creativity and a belief in a better future. Hope is cultivated during grief work when new goals come to mind, coupled with a determination that the goal can be reached. During the acute time of grief, hope may exist as a spark, rather than a flame. It is based on probability, possibility, and the perception of a favorable outcome. It is rare that a survivor will feel completely hopeless, even though feelings of desperation and deprivation may be painfully figural.

The psychologist Charles Snyder (1994) provides a lively, viable definition of hope. He reports hope as the sum of the mental willpower and 'way power' an individual has for goals. Included in his definition are three underlying concepts. The first relates to goals as objects, experiences, or outcomes that are imagined and desired. Hopeful goals fall somewhere between an impossibility and a sure thing. Such a definition underlines that hope is based on probability and prediction. The second concept refers to willpower as the driving force in hopeful thinking. Willpower draws on the perception of the desired goal as well as personal energy and motivation. It is amplified by how well the goal is understood and appreciated. Finally, the third concept is one that Snyder refers to as "way power," which reflects the mental plans or road maps that guide hopeful thought. It is the ability to prioritize the steps necessary to plan through a goal and to map out a stepwise course. Way power is where "the rubber meets the road" in terms of the actualization of realistic possibilities.

There are several specific distinctions to be made when describing the processes of hope. False hope is based on fantasies or impossible outcomes, and is likely to be harmful. Psychologists describe this as "magical thinking," defined as the belief that an object, action or circumstance *not logically related* to a course of events can influence its outcome. In other words, stepping on a crack cannot, given what is known about the principles of causal relations, have any direct effect on the probability of your mother breaking her back. Those who live in fear of such a tragedy are engaging in magical thinking and behaving irrationally. True hope may hold a distant or improbable goal, but one that is nevertheless plausible in its favorable outcome. True hope is also significantly different from optimism. Hope entails pathways and thoughts about an intended goal. Optimism leads an individual to expect the best, but it does not necessarily provide for critical thinking about how to arrive at the improved future. Hope must be understood in its sense of effectiveness in the pursuit of goals. The emotions of happiness, joy, courage, and the feeling of empowerment correspond to hope and deepen the sense of understanding of likelihood of a successful outcome. The higher the probability of reaching a desired outcome, the more grounded the sense of hope.

ANXIETY

Fear and anxiety are familiar experiences and involve recurrent existential themes for those who are grieving. Psychologically, anxiety is viewed as a dynamic energy, with the power to drive, distort, or defend against what is perceived as a reality. In theology, anxiety has been interpreted as resulting from a divine disconnection, i.e., the experience of being separated from God's grace. Philosophically, anxiety is seen as a positive state, since it is the mark of a person exercising personal freedom and responsibility to choose an authentic life.

Anxiety is characterized by a feeling of foreboding, accompanied by physical arousal. When a person experiences anxiety, a behavioral alarm is sounded to escape and avoid the origin of the threat, but without accompanying action. Somatic responses heighten the energy and edginess and include muscle tension, hypervigilance, and shortness of breath. Psychologically, anxiety musters as a sense of apprehension and uneasiness, stemming from the anticipation and perception of danger, either internal (self-induced) or external, coming from the environment (APA, 2007). In grief, anxiety varies in intensity, duration, and frequency: The anxious experience is out of proportion to the actual likelihood or impact of the feared event. Worrisome thoughts interfere with attention to tasks at hand. Anxiety is difficult to stop.

Anxiety is different from fear. While there are similarities and overlaps, fear is action oriented, particularly toward escape. It also has an avoidance motive. Fear motivates the flight-or-flight mechanism in the psyche. Anxiety, however, is characterized by a generalized lack of resolution, a sense of undirected energy, and the perception of an abstract threat that an individual "cannot put [their] finger on." The anxiety that musters in grief is painful because there is no way of escaping the reality of the loss. The worry accompanying grief-related anxiety is marked by uncontrollable, distressing chains of thoughts and images that are difficult to interrupt. The worries appear to involve thoughts more than images (Borkovec & Inz, 1990), which make the ability to grasp and hold onto what is alarming more elusive.

As an individual grieves, such manifest anxiety rarely seems reasonable. At its most basic level, anxiety is designed to alert an individual to the potential for danger. At its best, it functions to heighten the senses in order to effectively locate a threat. When grieving, threats are amorphous, vague, and ambiguous. What is detected as threatening is not anticipatory; the loss has already occurred. When the threat is not effectively addressed or understood, the individual spins. The author Ruth Gendler spoke of anxiety in this way. "Anxiety is secretive. He does not trust anyone, not even his friends. Worry. Terror. Doubt, and Panic. He has a way of glombing onto your skin like smog, and then you feel unclean. He likes to visit me late at night when I am alone and exhausted. I have never slept with him, but he kissed me on the forehead once, and I had a headache for two years. He is sure a nuisance to get out of the house. He has no respect for locks or curtains or doors. I speak from experience. It takes cunning to get rid of him, a combination of anger, humor, and self-respect" (1988, p. 13).

LOVE

The power of love cannot be underestimated in the grieving process, nor is it simple to define. Love in its various forms acts as a primary facilitator of interpersonal relationships. The word "love" has a variety of related but distinct meanings in different contexts. Cultural differences in conceptualizing love make it even more difficult to establish a universal definition. Most believe that love is a cognitive and social phenomenon, containing three components: intimacy, commitment, and passion (Sternberg, 1986). Intimacy is a form in which people share confidences and various details of personal life, and is usually demonstrated in friendships and romantic love. Commitment involves the expectation of longevity. Passion is the energy that serves to "glue" the loving relationship. Involved in these three components are complex appraisals or apprehensions, subjective feelings, expressions, physiological processes, and behavioral demonstrations of affection and tenderness. In loving relationships, there is the sense of being intertwined and linked in favorable, positive ways.

The connections of love and grief can be conceived as a form of attachment. As discussed in Chapter 2, attachment is an affectional tie between one's inner self and another person or thing. Children's early patterns of attachment influence their adult attachments. An elaborate and full discussion of attachment theory is beyond the scope of this book. Summarily, attachment begins occurring in infancy in the absence of the reinforcement of biological needs, e.g., food. The baby attaches to another to provide safety and security. Early in life, attachments are directed toward a few specific individuals. These attachments tend to endure throughout time. Children are likely to become more securely attached to their parents when allowed to be affectionate and independent. These children should mature into secure adults who are comfortable with intimacy and are able to trust and depend on those they care for. Children become anxious and ambivalent if they have learned to be clingy and dependent, fearful of being smothered or restrained, or both by parental figures. Such children may grow into adult life carrying this anxiety, which manifests as the threat of abandonment. Children who were indeed abandoned early on tend to grow into avoidant adults, feeling significant discomfort at any notion of dependence on others.

The intensity of grief, which is defined by the loss of the attachment bond, is dependent on several factors. The first is the strength of the attachment, and is proportionate to the intensity of the relationship between the survivor and deceased. The second is related to the security of the attachment, which raises the question "How necessary was the deceased for the survivor's sense of well-being?" The third is highly dependent on the ambivalence found in the relationship. In any enduring relationship, there are co-existing positive and negative feelings. As one fellow described his relationship with a deceased friend, "We knew the good, the bad, and the ugly about each other. We also had a lot of conflict with each other, primarily because we were so honest. We simply weren't nice in our friendship. This was the best part of what we had. There were many times that I had to take the thirty thousand foot perspective when considering our relationship. The ambivalence gave me a chance to evaluate our friendship, and I truly miss that." "Well," he sighed and laughed, "at least most days."

Loving attachments make life worth living. Attachment ensures that the survivor will feel pain in the face of loss. The more the attachment is deeply felt, the more effect the presence of death brings. As another woman said about her relationship with a favorite aunt, "The higher you go, the harder you fall. I scaled the heights of life with my aunt, and when she was no longer able to travel with me, I really hurt. I was so happy to have her from childhood into my adult life, but I wanted her to live longer – specifically, the rest of my life. I know it was wishful thinking, but I wanted her to be at every milestone. Throughout my life, I came to rely on my aunt for love, warmth, humor, and intelligence. She was a constant in my life. It is really interesting to me, now that she has died, that she continues to be a constant, just now in her death as much as she was in my life. We were connected at the hip while she was alive. Now, as I grieve, we are connected at the heart and in my memories of her."

DEFENSE MECHANISMS, VULNERABILITY, AND SELF-PROTECTION

Grief and loss are characterized by the vulnerability of the survivor. Beginning with Kübler-Ross and her colleagues' writings and moving forward into contemporary study, grief is discussed as a raw experience, psychologically similar to a sunburn. Even for those wishing to offer comfort and solace, touching those who grieve is painful and to be approached with caution and care. A death bounces the bereaved out of everyday experience and into a state of emotional conflict, anxiety, and tension as the loss is addressed, understood, and incorporated.

Early psychoanalytic theories, beginning with the writings of Freud, use the model of the id, ego, and superego to describe the components of human personality. The ego, tempered by the superego, is that conscious part that acts as a mediator between the instinctual drives of the unconscious id and the social environment. The ego uses components called defense mechanisms to cover the rawness of the id, which if left unchecked, lead a person into socially unacceptable behavior. These defense mechanisms function as psychological clothing to help those who grieve to metaphorically dress for the weather.

The death of a loved one causes tension. Most people feel driven to reduce the tension, which is caused by anxiety. Psychoanalytic theory identifies three different types of anxiety. Reality anxiety is the basic form and is based on fears of real and possible events, such as the concern that a middle-aged son might feel when his father dies of a heart attack. He might say, "There may be a genetic link to cardiac problems in my family. I should do something to check it out." The most common way of reducing this type of tension is to leave the threatening situation. The son might continue to think, saying "I'm still pretty healthy, though, so I have plenty of time to do get a physical."

Neurotic anxiety comes from an unconscious fear that the basic impulses of the id will take control of the person, leading to exposure and punishment. A woman described this sense of anxiety during her husband's funeral, saying, "I feel like I wanted to yell at everyone to pay attention to what they have in their marriages – now. They won't be able to get it back after their spouse is gone!" Such neurotic anxiety is accompanied by a third type, known as moral anxiety, which is based on the fear of violating social values and moral codes. It appears in the feelings of guilt and shame. The woman continued, "I was barely able to stop myself from screaming. I thought, if I get on my soapbox in the middle of the room, people would think I'm crazy. I probably am, but I'd just as soon not be held up as an example of the town madwoman."

When anxiety occurs, the mind initially responds by increasing problem-solving thinking and searching for rational ways to escape the threatening situation. When there is no reasonable exit, a range of defense mechanisms are triggered. Defense mechanisms are a part of everyday life and are used to provide self-deceptions that are protective from unacceptable instinctive desires. All defense mechanisms share two common properties: They appear unconsciously and out of rational awareness and they tend to distort, transform, or otherwise falsify reality. Such distortions of reality change perceptions, allowing for a lessening of anxiety. As a result, there is a corresponding reduction in the amount of tension that is felt.

Why is this important in the discussion of grief work? People tend to develop habitual modes and methods of managing stress and anxiety. Every individual has a preferred way for coping with upsetting emotional states. For the most part, these tried-and-true methods help a person manage and diffuse anxiety. Some methods work better than others. In the presence of a new situation, i.e., the death of a loved one, a person's typical coping strategies and defensive styles may be under-developed and cause more problems than they solve.

There is a relationship between emotional maturity, preferred defensive strategies, and coping methods. Less emotionally mature people tend to prefer rather primitive and inefficient mechanisms, while more mature individuals lean toward more sophisticated and useful methods. The less mature mechanisms tend to hold the common thread of reactivity rather premeditation; they are generally not well thought out. With increasing maturity and sophistication, the individual operates from an increasingly conscious stance and becomes more proactive and deliberate when responding to and coping with anxiety. The most primitive defense mechanisms rely on blatant misrepresentation or outright ignoring of reality in order to function. These mechanisms function in the mind and social situations so that emotion trumps reason and impulsivity rules the day. Children naturally use primitive defenses. With age and maturation, the individual is held to a higher standard of what is reasonable.

The primitive defense mechanism of denial seems to go hand-in-hand with grief. It underlies many of the other, more sophisticated defenses. When denial is employed, there is a simple refusal or inability to accept some aspect of immediate reality. It is characterized by the response of "No, that can't be!" when initially hearing about an unexpected death. Denial can be beneficial as an initial protective response. When a person says, "this really isn't happening," the defense is allowing necessary time for a gathering of psychological wits required to meet the demands of the death. In the long run, though, denial prevents the individual from incorporating unpleasant information about the self, the reality of day-to-day experience, and can have potentially destructive consequences.

Regression is one step up from denial on the ladder of defense mechanism sophistication. In regression, old childhood emotional states of unconscious fears, anxieties, and angst reappear. As has been noted, when under stress, people tend to revert back to their most primitive, unconscious, and tried-and-true means of handling a situation. Particularly in the presence of death, unmet dependency needs tend to rear their ugly head. The problem with regression emerges when childhood needs become child-ish (when observed in an adult), serving to frustrate those who grieve and irritate those who try to soothe.

Displacement is the defense mechanism allowing an individual to transfer original feelings (usually anger) away from its true target and onto a safer person or circumstance. During grief, many people find it difficult to be upset with the deceased, so it seems reasonable to shift the feelings to someone else or to a more socially acceptable situation. Following the death of her husband who lingered during a long illness, a woman complained mightily about the chaplain who called to notify her. "I'll never get over how wrong he did the whole thing. He shouldn't have surprised me. It was hard enough dealing with John's illness without having it sprung on me that he died when I wasn't there."

At the mature end of the defense mechanism spectrum are those defined by a more ambivalent relationship with reality. Using better coping strategies, reality is ultimately recognized to a larger extent, even if it is put off or avoided. Defensively, overwhelming feelings or thoughts about a death can be handled by isolating their meaning from feelings. This is known as intellectualization. For example, it is entirely possible that readers of this text will be coping with the recent death of a parent and will seek to understand the different processes of grief from an academic point of view. Rationalization is similar to intellectualization, but involves dealing with a piece of bad behavior rather than converting a painful or negative emotion into a more neutral set of thoughts. Rationalization shores up insecurity or remorse after an "oops" moment. For example, it is easier to blame someone else rather than to feel shame or embarrassment after a loss of temper. Rationalization is the "it wasn't my fault" stance.

Repression is a milder form of denial and is characterized by the management of uncomfortable feelings and thoughts by admitting to the state of distress while distancing from it. As a woman said, "If I try not to think about it long enough, it eventually will go away."

Defense mechanisms are among the most common ways to cope with unpleasant emotions. They come into play and are applied in a wide variety of situations when an individual feels anxious and uncertain. The more mature defense mechanisms of intellectualization, repression, and rationalization are probably the most adaptive, keeping reality at arm's length until it can seep into the conscious realm of experience.

COGNITIVE DISSONANCE AND GRIEF

People tend to seek consistency in their beliefs and perceptions. A cognition is the mental process of knowing something – a thought, value, fact, or emotion. Most cognitions operate independently and have little or nothing to do with one another. The few that do correspond are either harmonious with one another, which feels good, or not harmonious, which creates anxiety. When a tried-and-true belief conflicts with another previously held belief, the term cognitive dissonance is used to describe the feeling of discomfort that results from holding the two in close proximity. When there is a discrepancy between beliefs and behaviors, something must change in order to eliminate or reduce the dissonance. This is where the problem arises, particularly in the presence of grief and loss.

Consider this story: A man was actively involved with chemotherapy and radiation therapy to fight a virulent, malignant lung cancer. He had been told that his prognosis was grim, and that the treatment was dreadful. Family members belonged to a local Evangelical Christian community, and prayed for a miracle. Six weeks into the torturous treatment, scans revealed no evidence of the tumors. Despite attempts by the oncologist and treatment team to otherwise instruct the patient and family, a miracle was pronounced by the faith community – the tumors were "gone" and a miracle had indeed happened. The treatment was stopped. Several weeks later, another scan revealed further metastasis, much to the distress of the patient, his family, and his church.

Cognitive dissonance plays a role in value judgments, decisions, and evaluations. Consider the example of the deceased "pillar of the community" who, during the funeral rites and rituals, was revealed to be a closet alcoholic and prescription drug abuser who had neglected his family for many years. Such conflicting knowledge created uncomfortable tension among the bereaved who found it difficult to hold such discordant thoughts about the deceased at the same time. Dissonance increases with the importance of the subject, how strongly the dissonant thoughts conflict, and the inability to rationalize or explain away the conflict. It is a powerful motivator which will lead an individual to change one or the other of the conflicting beliefs or actions. The tension must be released, and happens in one of three ways: Behavior is changed, justified by changing the belief, or by new cognitions added to those currently operating. A friend of the closeted alcoholic said, "I'm just not going to believe that he could've been such a good man to us and a drunk behind closed doors. I'm afraid his children must have some kind of unfinished business or axes to grind with each other. I don't know why they have to say these things now that he's gone."

As noted, an individual will attempt to do away with cognitive dissonance in several ways. One way is to ignore it. A pretense of defense is enacted to shield the psyche from the conflict. It is not unusual for a bereaved individual to engage in magical thinking that permits momentary relief from the reality of the physical absence of the deceased. One man said of his recently deceased wife, "I just kept thinking she'd walk through the door. I could not wrap my brain around the idea that she would never come back." A second way is to alter the thought's importance. By lessening the importance of one of the conflicting thoughts, there is less difficulty with it. Another friend of the deceased community pillar said, "It really isn't important if he was alcoholic. Look what he did for the greater good. It doesn't seem to me like his family suffered too much, either." A third way to deal with cognitive dissonance is to create new cognitions that will overcome the problem, such as saying, "It was God's will that John was taken before his time. Heaven needed him more than we did."

SPIRITUALITY AND DEATH

The reconciliation of the cognitive dissonance involved in the above example underlines that death is commonly characterized as a transformational event involving both physical change and spiritual fulfillment. Losses of any kind reconfigure an individual's beliefs about how life is lived. This primary belief, that spiritual beliefs and practices qualitatively and quantitatively impact death and grief, is held in many of the world's religions. The belief calls the question regarding spirituality and death: "How may we understand spirituality and its involvement with psychological experience? What empirical relationships exist between spirituality and mortality? What significance may spiritual belief provide for the individuals and their family as they encounter death?" (Vondros & White, 2006)

In 1971, the White House Council on Aging defined spiritual concerns as "the human need to deal with sociocultural deprivations, anxieties, and fears, death and dying, personality integration, self-image, personal dignity, social alienation, and philosophy of life" (Corless, 1986, p. 8). Spiritual concerns were distinguished from spiritual needs, noted as "factors necessary to establish and maintain a relationship with God, or some transcendental reality, however that reality is defined by the individual." Spiritual well-being was further defined as "the affirmation of life in a relationship with God, self, community, and environment that nurtures and celebrates wholeness" (Ellerhorhost-Ryan, 1985, p. 93). These are broad, encompassing descriptions of the term spirituality that extend much further than religiosity or denominationalism. While the term spiritual is commonly identified with religion, its roots are found elsewhere. The word spirit comes from the Greek origin meaning breath. As time passed, it became identified as the spirit with living things and is now used to describe the specialness and uniqueness of the human person. Twentieth century philosophers have come to speak of the term spirit as "the expression of the inexpressible" (Martain, 1966).

Spirituality and religion are quite different constructs. Spirituality is defined as a personal relationship with the transcendent, with a primary focus on making meaning of the experiences in life and death. In contrast, religion is the practice of spirituality and includes beliefs, activities, and language that afford the search for the transcendent. Spirituality is marked by knowledge and the wish to know more, in spite of what is already known. This wish for knowledge is quickly followed by a quest to feel good and find comfort in the world. Comfort is defined by individual and collective senses of ethic and mortality and indicative of individual and communal character.

The most fundamental example of the spiritual nature of a person lies in the ability to self-determine. Individuals make sense out of life through decisions and actions. This describes how a person is known at the deepest and most intimate levels of self. Spirituality is expressed through decision making, which establishes a world of values and the communication of that private world to others. "Perhaps, in the long run, maturity in our lives consists in taking seriously the fact that things do not just happen, that each of us has a responsibility to effect our vision of reality" (Morgan, 1993, p. 8). Not everyone may express a religious orientation, but those who seek transcendent meaning can be considered to have a sense of spirituality. Some believe that spirituality is the lived experience and others believe that it is within each individual with a set course that must simply be followed. While expressed differently, each person's spirituality is a way of reconnecting the individual with the transcendent. The spirit of a person is that which addresses the need to find satisfactory answers to ultimate questions about the meaning of life, illness, and death. The spirit itself is concerned with deep relationships to self, others, and the Divine.

The writer J.D. Morgan continues,

> The spiritual nature of the person encompasses the idea that each of us is a part of a larger whole. We find not only the meaning in our lives in that larger whole but have some obligation to it. This I think is what is meant by religion. In this sense, religious applies not only to the usual western or eastern religions, but also includes philosophies and other movements in which persons find meaning in their lives. Each person must ask what it is that gives meaning to life, and whether whatever is chosen will be a defense against those bad times, such as death and bereavement, that come into each life. We cannot escape from our spirituality. Even Camus' call to live absurdly, as though there were no values, as though life were totally meaningless, is a call to exercise our spirituality. We can live absurdly, reject all values only by becoming conscious of the power to think and the power to will, the root of our spirituality (1993, p. 8).

In the consideration of spirituality and grief, relationships are viewed as a significant part of the created order to the world. Most people hold a sense of timelessness in their understanding of what it means to "be." "The mystery of existence, awe and joy before the natural order, a sense of the sublime in the manifestations of our loves, and a sure confidence in the continuity through children create in many a sense of union with the infinite and immortal" (Mermann, 1992, p. 138). The philosopher Kierkegaard described this sense of spirituality in his famous phrase 'leap of faith', which was defined as the intellectual characteristics of evidence of the spirit in the lives of others, personal commitment, and loyalty. In this view, the leap of faith is an orienting process during grief, and holds hope for transcendence and redemption. As Mermann (1992) notes, "There are the three hopes inherent in faith: it holds us on our proper course despite the trials and tribulations of all life; it leads us to an understanding of self and cosmos that exceeds the mundane; it can make our lives objects of value and respect" (p. 138).

In the presence of loss, a natural search for a spiritual unity runs as a common thread through personal history. People take many and varied paths, though the search for answers to deeply felt questions about the mysteries of existence are magnified and heightened by death and dying. The pain and suffering associated with loss are understood by many as an enlightening part of the journey made toward a developing concept of God. A mature construct of the Divine provides the base and power for the benefits of faith, including sophisticated emotions, competent judgment, and revealing insight. Again, the writer Alan Mermann speaks. "Does life have meaning? The shadow of death sweeps away easy answers and supports the alternative of considering anew the measured thought of the past about this human journey. This question posits a place for the life of the spirit as enricher of the life that is lived until death" (1992, p. 140).

There is no single religious understanding of the human experience in living and dying. Beliefs about the specifics of the spirit and faith are as diverse and contradictory as are any other human activities. Death is the end of life as it can be known. It is inevitable and not to be feared but to be accepted as the closing out of one form of being in hope of another eternal existence in the Universal or Divine. The nature and form of that new life cannot be known, but remain a mystery beyond understanding and comprehension. Spirituality provides a grounding orientation and affords an opportunity to develop meaning and purpose for life and death, as well as a sense of integrity about how one has lived. Therefore, spiritual beliefs provide an interpretive meaning of the dying and grieving process and offer comfort to the individual, family, and community.

Spirituality can be easily overlooked or compromised in grief, yet everyone has a spiritual component, even those who find the very word objectionable or irrelevant. Within the person, there is a desire to believe, trust, and hope. In grief, the gifts bearing these attributes may, at least for a time, appear strangled by the pain of loss. Healthy spirituality is affirming, meets sorrow, and offers an expression of community when an individual is confused, hurt, or disappointed. It can provide an antidote to abandonment, or as one man said, "…at least a pathway through it." Healthy spirituality acknowledges that things happen for many reasons, and sometimes for no reason at all. Healthy spirituality invites: "…meeting us where we are, as we are, not where others, including religion determine where we should be" (Gilbert, 2006, p. 10). Loss can be exceedingly painful. Spiritual pathways, in any religion as well in no particularly defined religious expression, should move a person from pain to a measure of redemption and comfort, which facilitate healthier grieving.

Alice Cullinan (1993) writes,

> …spirituality is concerned with the transcendental, inspirational, and existential ways of being human and living one's life. Caregivers working with the bereaved are urged to be sensitive to the interrelationship of mental, emotional, and physical responses of the spiritually-oriented bereaved who will want to give spiritual questions time and attention. A person's spiritual nature is seen revealing itself in widely differing religious and philosophical beliefs and practices depending on race, sex, class, spirituality, ethnic heritage, and prior experience…Spirituality is viewed as being expressed and enhanced in a broad range of opportunities for expressing and enhancing one's relationship with the Divine: formal and informal, in religious and secular symbols, rituals, practices, patterns and gestures, art forms, prayers and meditations (p. 198).

IV

Facilitating the Natural Process of Grief

I do not believe that sheer suffering teaches. If suffering alone taught, all the world would be wise, since everyone suffers. To suffering must be added mourning, understanding, patience, love, openness, and the willingness to remain vulnerable.

Ann Morrow Lindbergh

Grief is the response to loss. It is distress marked by a keen, sharp mental suffering. Typically, the more significant the loss, the more intense is the grief. While the concept is easy to describe, grief is a complex entity in itself. It presents differently in everyone through variances in intensity, complexity, duration, and the properties presenting in individual experience. The terms grief counseling and grief therapy are reserved for helping another work through this process, either following the death of a loved one or with major life changes that trigger feelings of grief, e.g., divorce, through one-on-one or group interventions. The goal of such a course of treatment is to facilitate the individual's movement through a typically uncomplicated process to the point of a healthy resolution of grief within a reasonable, though undetermined, amount of time.

Elisabeth Kübler-Ross' work changed the nature of the approach to grief facilitation. Because of her work, contemporary grief counselors are now taught to see the bereaved as teachers. Grief is idiosyncratic and subjective, and significantly shaped by familial, community, and ethnic cultures. Allowing for the impact of Kübler-Ross's thought, researchers and clinicians have progressively moved away from the conventional view that grief moves through orderly and predictable stages. The current zeitgeist of grief counseling is that there is no typical response to a loss, nor a "normal" timeline for grieving. However, there are common symptoms and a wide range of expected emotions and behaviors associated with grief. It is multi-faceted and includes physical, social, and spiritual aspects in addition to the affective and behavioral shifts associated with loss. The process is natural and most people move through an uncomplicated process of grief without the need for therapeutic intervention. There are times, though, that an individual may become sufficiently disabled by grief and become overwhelmed with the loss. Preferred coping styles, skills, and responses can shut down. This is where grief facilitation/counseling has merit as it aids in processing the expression of emotion and thought about the loss, which typically includes a complex mix of sadness, loneliness, guilt, and confusion.

GOALS AND PROCESSES OF GRIEF COUNSELING

Grief counseling and therapy consist of clearing psychological space for healing. Many people who grieve feel as though they are strangers in a strange land, in unknown territory, and in need of assistance to create the sense of safety needed for exploration and understanding of the loss. Much of grief work is facilitated by social support. This suggests that practitioners of grief counseling serve a primary function as witness to a very personal process, allowing the individual who mourns to teach the therapist about the experience of loss (rather than the counselor who constructs a set of goals or expectations that must be met and achieved). This stance is fundamentally different from traditional efficacy-based counseling and psychotherapy approaches; grief counseling and therapy comes from more of a developmental or evolutionary frame of reference. These processes are difficult to objectify in standard clinical case formularies.

A graduate student, during a master's level course on grief and bereavement, asked her teacher, "How can you work with so many grieving people and maintain your sense of self?" The teacher answered, "Sloppily, or not at all." Maybe the answer was given with tongue-in-cheek, but a truer statement could not have been spoken. Even with all of the study about grief and techniques of counseling and therapy, there are no experts in this work. Author John Welshons said, "So there is no way to apply systems, rules or emotional road maps. Our job is to be a presence, rather than a savior. A companion, rather than a leader. A friend, rather than a teacher" (2002, p. 159). While most counseling professionals would take exception to the therapeutic role of "the friendly visitor," the point is well taken: Grief facilitation requires the therapist to work in a side-by-side, egalitarian frame examining the process as a work-in-progress, rather than manipulating a set of symptoms that are to be cured.

The grief writer Alan Wolfelt calls this process, in a term that harkens to Welshons' writing, "companioning." Wolfelt elaborates on this companioning approach to grief counseling with the following statements:

- Companioning is about honoring the spirit; it is not about focusing on the intellect.
- Companioning is about curiosity; it is not about expertise.
- Companioning is about learning from other; it is not about teaching them.
- Companioning is about walking alongside; it is not about leading.
- Companioning is about being still; it not about frantic movement forward.
- Companioning is about discovering the gifts of sacred silence; it is not about filling every painful moment with words.
- Companioning is about listening with the heart; it is not about analyzing with the head.
- Companioning is about bearing witness to the struggles of others; it is not about directing those struggles.
- Companioning is about being present to another person's pain; it is not about taking away the pain.
- Companioning is about respecting disorder and confusion; it is not about imposing order and logic.
- Companioning is about going to the wilderness of the soul with another human being; it is not about thinking you are responsible for finding the way out (1998, p. 6).

The essence of grief counseling is found in the validation of experience. Grieving individuals need and want on-going reassurance that the felt sense of grief is typical and to be expected. Sensitivity to the unique ways that grief presents is crucial, as is assisting in understanding and recognizing the responses, reactions, and interpretations made to the loss. The overarching goal of grief counseling is to help the bereaved move toward integration of the loss by facilitating conversation and discussion about the death, the relationship between the survivor and deceased, and the circumstances surrounding end-of-life care and the corresponding changes exacted in the life of the survivor. Encouragement of descriptions of feeling states encompassing the loss become figural during grief counseling. Two critical elements of grief counseling include helping the bereaved to understand their personal coping behaviors and styles and identifying coping mechanisms that are problematic or unhealthy. Without attention to these elements, the individual may continue or deepen unhealthy patterns that would require more intense or intrusive intervention.

As noted, there is no timetable for processing loss. Grief reconciliation and integration depend on multiple factors confronting the individual in the context of daily living. An elderly man, grieving the loss of his wife of many years said, "There are days that I think I will die without her. But, I just keep on living. I don't know if this is a good thing or a bad thing, I just know that life keeps coming, in spite of her death." This fellow's experience is common and familiar: Grief involves many changes in the life of the individual. Therefore, it is likely that reactions will change over time.

What becomes figural are the reactions following the loss. Grief is a period of adaptation and transitions. It is the whole person facing the forced change, even though many who grieve report feeling fragmented and cut off from parts of the self. As one man said, "I felt like I was in a maze. Sometimes I could see where I was going, other times I was blind." Adapting to such a maze takes an indeterminable amount of time. The man in the maze continued, saying, "It just takes as long as it needs to take. People tell me I should be over by now. They just don't know that I'll never get 'over it.' The best I can do it learn to live with it." The individual's circumstances in life, coping mechanisms, and spiritual/philosophical beliefs all contribute to the outcome, warranting exploration for sufficiency and balance.

Resolution of grief includes a goal of learning to accept that loss is not a process leading to closure, but one of integration. A woman described this process as "…a journey. I thought all of the Kübler-Ross stages were tasks and, Lord only knows, I tried to accomplish them. The harder I tried, the more frustrated I felt. I couldn't do anything to 'get better.' While I was in therapy, I realized that the loss was a part of my life. I had to learn to take it in, not try and separate myself from it. It took a great deal of presence, but I did learn that the loss had emotional, behavioral, cognitive, and spiritual aspects…all that I needed to account for. The death of my beloved touched every part of my body, heart, and soul. I am still touched in profound ways, just without as much pain as I used to feel."

Such is the general process for grief facilitation. With a good roadmap, a grief counselor can help guide each individual's process in a distinct, helpful fashion. In many ways, the grief counselor serves as a navigator through the territory of loss. As metaphorical space is cleared for this personal journey, progress is made by marking the integration of the loss into the survivor's day-to-day experience.

Initially, the loss must be actualized. A significant loss, even when expected and anticipated, is considered a foreign experience. Most people do not have regular experience with death and dying. If not unique in a person's life, it is unusual and infrequent. Psychologically, "taking in" this type of experience requires time to incorporate and accommodate. Fortunately, there are natural unconscious ways that manifest, allowing the individual to acknowledge the truth and fact of the reality of the death over time. They are protective mechanisms called defenses, which have been discussed earlier. As noted, defense mechanisms serve to reduce internal tension caused by anxiety that has become too painful to hold. The defenses are psychological strategies brought into play by the unconscious mind to manipulate, deny, or distort reality sufficiently so the individual can maintain a socially acceptable self-image or self-schema. They allow the individual to progressively incorporate 'truth' while maintaining a sense of balance in an upset world.

A thoughtful fellow described this process in himself. He said, "It took me a while to realize the impact of the loss. When it finally came to me, I fell in love with the word 'realize.' I began to see the death of my sweet wife with 'real eyes.' For a while, I was into magical thinking. I thought and really believed she might come back from a long trip. Then there were times I heard her moving through the house, and quite honestly, most of the time I just pretended that she wasn't dead. None of it worked in the long run, but as I look back, I can see that I needed every trick in the book just to make sense out of the fact of her death. Some people said that I was stuck in denial. Nothing could be further from the truth. I needed every ounce of denial that I mustered. It served me well. I look back on the time and it seems a little foolish, but I'm not going to be too hard on myself." Only when the bereaved fail to actualize the loss does the process become complicated or should defensiveness be alarming.

Multiple waves of potent affect are generated by the death of a loved one. Oftentimes, these feelings are elusive, hard to identify, and manifest primarily as anxiety or alarm. The grief counselor serves a valuable purpose by helping the survivor identify and express such a myriad of feelings in a fashion that feels safe and valid. Grief is not social, so facilitating such emotional expression often violates social norms of propriety. The grief counselor normalizes the syncopation of the mourner's needs and wishes to be with and apart from others, and aids in validating the wide swings involved in the need for social contact and distance. A woman described her experience following the death of an adult child. "It was around the holidays, and people told me that I should "get out more." I do believe they had my best interests at heart. But I just couldn't commit. I went to a luncheon one day and just had to leave. I thought I would scream if I had to talk about trivialities or make any more small talk. Fortunately, I had some therapy help to talk this through. My counselor and I decided that I would ask for all invitations to be issued, but that I would tell people that they should not worry if I accepted, refused, or reneged. Once I explained how unpredictable I was, people gave me lots of latitude. I was able to do what I wanted at the time, and didn't need to worry about planning whether I'd be good company or not."

Concurrent to the emotional turmoil of death is the requirement that the survivor continue to prioritize the day-to-day tasks that are necessary for living and basic subsistence. Grief can be overwhelming. One fellow said, "It stopped me dead in my tracks." A grief counselor can assist in the sorting process of what is more or less important in managing the day. The fellow continued. "There were days that I just wanted to sleep. I was going to work, because I knew that I had to. But my personal life just stopped. I stopped opening the mail, didn't clean my house, and just could have cared less about things. The hospice bereavement coordinator got me into a widower's group, and that was helpful. There were many times that I needed someone to hold my hand just to help me take the next step." This gentleman's experience is not unusual. Such time management feels intrusive, and most people in the bereaved's social circles are unable or unwilling to intrude in such personal ways.

Grief counselors are reminded that the death of a loved one, while primary, is not the only loss experienced. Death is rarely simple; it involves multiple levels and layers of loss, including changes in status, income, circumstance, and social arrangement. One older woman said, "I had never been the 'third wheel' before. We had great couples' friends, and after my husband died, all of our friends continued to care for me, invite me, and want to be with me. I felt them loving me, but I also felt like an outsider, an intruder, and a bother more than anything else. Now, how do you tell this to people who love you and want the best for you? I really needed the grief counselor to help me sort this out. I originally went to see her to help me understand some of the financial things that I needed to deal with. She really was able to listen and help me realize how many losses were tied up in my husband's death. Who knew? I certainly didn't."

Many who grieve, particularly early in the experience of loss, are alarmed by "good" days. As noted in an earlier chapter, relief is a part of the oscillating wave-like nature of grief. One grief counselor described the process as "diving deep and resurfacing." Those grieving frequently describe surprise and feel guilty in the presence of relief and respite. To catch one's psychological breath is an unexpected, though natural part of the grieving process, and warrants validation as an acceptable part of the process. Such relief provides the mourner to progressively gain bits of perspective to the death and the relationship with the deceased. The perspective is necessary to integrate the loss, so the coming of relief is desirable on many levels of experience.

THE ASSUMPTIVE WORLD

These major secondary losses, including changes in socioeconomic status, loss of family stability, and loss of belief or confidence in an established faith all impact the adjustment and reconciliation of the individual's loss. The assumptive world is shattered. An individual's *assumptive world* is the totality of assumptions about how the world works, e.g., what is safe/dangerous, important/unimportant, or good/bad. To assume is to believe without proof. Problems arise when the individual's assumptive world is out of harmony with reality. Because people like to understand and predict things, if assumptions are false, predictions are likely to be inaccurate. This results in frustration and a sense of failure. Without time to incorporate the changes due to the absence of the deceased, control, predictability, and security are lost, and the expectations and beliefs upon which the mourner has based his life are violated. As one fellow said, "I really thought I understood myself. After the death of my best friend, I lost my anchors. Things weren't predictable anymore. Even if they had been more of what I had come to expect, I wouldn't have trusted much of anything. There was a long period of time that I just felt lost."

The experience of grief must be processed in a highly subjective manner that allows for a flexing of coping and adaptive strategies and skills. Daily living continues while incorporating the loss of the relationship. As a result of the death, roles, expectations, opportunities, and hopes must be significantly altered, shifted, or given up. In grief, all personal adjustments potentially compromise the nature of the individual and speak to the transitional nature of grief. Ultimately, when the loss is acknowledged, newness will emerge. The sense of wholeness can be restored, but this happens slowly over time.

It has been noted that survivors of a significant loss find fundamental changes in social relationships. Often, there is a shift in relationship to family, friends, and acquaintances. Because many who are not closely related to the survivor are unsure about approaching during the grieving process, they stay away, stepping back in avoidance of the individual. One woman said, as she thought about a grieving church member, "I just didn't know what to do.... what to say....how to act. Time slipped away and I realized that I had just disconnected. One day I saw my friend in the grocery store and apologized, but the conversation was strained."

The survivor told the story about her friend. "I know she felt bad," she said, "but I didn't feel like helping her out of her quandary. We weren't close friends anyway, but we were in the same social circle. So many people haven't known what to do or say. I wish that 'nothing' had not been an option. Yes, things have changed. I'm not nearly as cheerful or outgoing as people may have known me, and I could use their energy right now. I've had to create new friends and a different social network than I had before my husband's death. I was angry about it for a while, but now I'm just resigned to the change."

Yearning

Those who experience a significant loss describe a psychological process colloquially known as yearning. It is described as the energy of longing, and drives an individual from one place to another, from one desire to a different one and then another one, in search of fulfillment to satisfy and finally silence the inner voice than never seems satisfied with anything. As one woman said, "...however hard I try, I still have this sense of longing and that something is missing."

As noted in the book *Isolated and Alone* (Rainer & Martin, 2013):

> The Greek word for longing is *thumos*, meaning the presence of life itself. It is the raw presence in the psyche that senses and feels, and in its original translation, is defined as the massed power of individual emotional being. Not only is it the energy of longing, but also the energy of passion and appetite. It moves without thought. So, when left to itself, it moves without reason. Feeling dislocated by grief heightens the tendency for this energy of longing to be experienced as pain. In pain, the individual is unable to see the self clearly, nor to attribute favorable meaning to experience. This, in turn, leaves the individual embittered and rejecting of all sources of support or relief. Because of its self-regulating tendency, the pain of yearning serves to distance and disconnect from any integration

of the grief experience. A fellow described this experience, saying, "The strange thing is that the negativity isn't the depression itself but in running from the depression. What I imagine I'm afraid of isn't what I'm really afraid of at all. I get afraid of the feeling of longing for something because I make no allowances for what I think or what I care for. The longing wants all of me and consumes me. I lose my sense of safety and want to look outside of myself. But then, there is nothing there because I am in such a remote place with myself" (p. 46-47).

A client elegantly described his experience with grief. "After my child died, I had to travel through the unknown to get to a place of certainty. I always thought that I took myself pretty seriously, but had to keep re-evaluating everything I had ever known. I didn't know whether to call myself a father anymore, how many children I should say that I have, the circumstances of my son's death – he died in a house fire…there were any number of places where I felt like I was stepping into quicksand. I knew that I needed help that would come in the form of something solid to hold onto, but there didn't seem to be anything. Friends, work, even time and space seemed temporary and elusive. I couldn't avoid the pain, but tried to avoid it at every turn. I was like a dog – chasing his tail and getting more and more upset that I couldn't catch it."

MAKING THE UNCONSCIOUS CONSCIOUS

Much of day-to-day life occurs as a result of generalizations that people make about their lives. In a psychological process called stimulus generalization, the mind groups similar stimuli together and responds to them in conditioned, predictable ways. Most of our personal habits are formed in this way and this is seen as an efficient and elegant process for energy conservation to prioritize what requires immediate attention. A common example of the stimulus generalization process is found in the ability to recognize emergency sirens as a call to alarm. A siren, regardless of its type of sound, activates the same internal message: "Stop, look, listen, and be ready to get out of the way!" These types of generalizations guide habits, governing and guiding behavior while working in the background of the mind, unless something significantly changes stimuli and activating events.

The death of a loved one is such a significant change, and certainly disrupts habit-driven behavior. In addition to behavior, humans have deep thoughts, feelings, and beliefs that stay in an internal dialogue and effect movement through the world. This deeper level is known as unconscious process. The unconscious works on problems and concerns while conscious attention is directed elsewhere. Both the conscious and unconscious work in concert to give weight to situations requiring priority and deliberation. The conscious mind employs working memory, sequential tasking, and summary judgments. It looks for congruence, shared assumptions about what is observed, and seeks to make "sense" out of incoming data and information. The unconscious works in a fundamentally different way.

The unconscious mind is a "story generator" (Grobstein, 2003). It functions to translate observations into personal implications and significance in and about life. Theories of the unconscious historically date back to Sigmund Freud's work and in recent decades, it has been quite fashionable to discredit and dismiss all of Freud's work. Some skepticism is valid: Freud did view human nature from a narrow frame of reference as a dreadful mix of unresolved psychosexual urges, misogynistic attitudes, and libidinal motivations. However, his work on the understanding of the unconscious continues to hold great fundamental value. By definition, the unconscious cannot be studied directly and must be inferred from behavior. Clinical evidence is required to translate the stories of the unconscious mind. The unconscious speaks in symbol, weave, and vague felt senses. It is hard to "pin down," which lends to the doubt of its validity. However, contemporary study of neuroscience has rekindled interest in the unconscious, specifically regarding the notion of causal decision-making processes. In its most general definition, the unconscious stores all personal experiences, memories, and repressed material. Needs and motivations that are out of awareness (therefore, inaccessible), are also outside the sphere of conscious control.

People tend to construct stories from the unconscious holding common themes that are used as personal life guides. Some people are optimists, some are pessimists. Some are gregarious and outgoing, while others are shy and retiring. These types of constructed self-definitions live in the unconscious, and maintain strength from relevant information gathered in day-to-day living. The unconscious generally guides available courses of action, prediction of outcomes, and payoffs for behaving in a certain way. The unconscious helps the individual choose a "best" course of action, i.e., what is most predictable and expected. One young fellow described the predictability of this process when he said, "Something will happen to mess this up. It always does. Even with the best laid plans, something always happens." His generally pessimistic attitude is based on stored and storied history that lends credibility to the expectations of how things will turn out.

When an individual is jarred out of habit-driven behavior, a sense of upset and an attempt to rebalance the system quickly follows. The unconscious signals and moves for a return to baseline. However, in the presence of loss, there is no such baseline. The deceased's physical presence and role functioning are permanently lost, and the relationship with the survivor shifts from what was literal to what will live as memorable. Such a change is uncomfortable, since it requires new choice points marked by frequent reminders of what is lost. Repetition of old habits, beliefs, and patterns of behavior must be exhausted before lasting change can occur. Because each individual has personal rhythms and patterns of the unconscious, time predictions for this "resetting" are unreliable and frustrating.

The author David Brooks calls the unconscious "the empire of emotion" and offers a lovely description of this inner realm in his book, *The Social Animal* (2011). He writes:

> If the conscious mind is like a general atop a platform, who sees the world from a distance and analyzes things linearly and linguistically, the unconscious mind is like a million little scouts. The scouts careen across the landscape, sending back a constant flow of signals and generating instant responses…These scouts coat things with emotional significance. They come across an old friend and send back a surge of affection. They descended into a dark cave and send back a surge of fear. Contact with a beautiful landscape produces a feeling of sublime elevation. Contact with a brilliant insight produces delight, while contact with unfairness produces righteous anger. Each perception has its own flavor, texture, and force, and reactions loop around the mind in a stream of sensations, impulses, judgment, and desires. These signals don't control our lives, but they shape our interpretation of the world and they guide us, like a spiritual GPS, as we chart our courses. If the general thinks in data and speaks in prose, the scouts crystallize with emotion, and their work is best expressed in stories, poetry, music, image, prayer, and myth (p. ix).

Insight is the mechanism for effective change. As an individual explores and examines the loss and the nature of the change it brings, there is a natural reshaping of psychological and environmental phenomena. The mind progressively adopts a "that was then, this is now" frame of reference, allowing for an assimilation of the loss. Once insight develops into the shift of perception, things are seen differently – not better or worse, but through a new set of eyes and experience.

This process happens naturally in the presence of loss, but can be thwarted by the individual. If there is too much anxiety, those defense mechanisms described earlier can postpone the active awareness of how things have changed. Maintenance of the defense mechanisms requires a good deal of psychological energy which can be easily wasted, ultimately leaving the individual feeling despairing. The grief counselor can help the bereaved to look at the loss from all sides, gaining perspective, which encourages personal interpretation of the changes and the meaning they bring to the day. Such adaptation moves the bereaved from a sense of feeling brittle to an appreciation of the flow of the unconscious process.

THE VALUE OF MEDICATION DURING GRIEF

Many people wonder if taking medication after the death of a loved one will help them sleep, feel less anxious, or take away sadness. Anti-anxiety and antidepressant medications affect the mind and behavior; they are known as psychotropic drugs. Regrettably, these medications do not bring about learning, coping, or integrating data and beliefs about the loss. Medications can occasionally be used to help an individual stabilize mood, particularly when there are secondary losses related to the inability to relate in a meaningful way to close people or when there is a loss of self-care, either physically or emotionally. However, their value in helping an individual integrate the death of a loved one is open for discussion and debate.

Researchers continue to examine the growing national concern that medicine often goes to people who should not be taking it. The availability of antidepressants – now the country's most commonly prescribed medication (Kotz, 2007) – suggests an increase in the diagnosis of depression. Grief experts believe that the SSRIs, such as Prozac, Paxil, and Zoloft, are commonly overused to treat sadness, the typical and healthy response to loss, which is easily misidentified as depression. Current diagnostics indicate that people grieving the death of a significant other can temporarily exhibit all of the signs of depression without having a mental disorder. For most people, after about two months of presenting symptoms, lingering signs are typically misclassified as symptoms of depression. Even though it has been noted that grief has its own timeline and proceeds at a deliberate pace, the diagnosis of depression can be made too quickly by primary care physicians who are not prone to consider the context of symptomatology. Depression is defined by five or more of a constellation of nine symptoms, ranging from depressed mood and suicidal thoughts to fatigue, insomnia, and difficulty concentrating. The symptoms should be constant and unremitting for more than two weeks, must be severe enough to interfere with social life and typical day-to-day rhythms, and not accounted for by a physical disorder (such as a low functioning thyroid). Prolonged depressive-like symptoms are common in those experiencing the pain of grief. It should be said again that many people who fit the clinical definition of depression are actually showing typical signs of sadness. These people are not mentally disordered and probably need more social and psychological support than medication.

Even when a congruent life circumstance is found to be at the root of the moodiness, physicians are reluctant to refer grieving individuals to counseling and therapy. Medication is an easier solution, especially when a quick fix is demanded. Antidepressants, however, are no panacea. While they can help numb the pain of sadness, they also dull all other feeling functions as well, such as joy, delight, and pleasure. There are multiple side-effects to these medicines, including decreased sexual energy and appetite, sleep difficulties, and particularly for young people – an initial increase in suicidal thoughts.

Medicating typical sadness can delay the healing process. Sadness provides focus. As one woman said, "The Prozac gave me a headache and I felt numb. It was as though there wasn't emotion to release, and I felt like I should be examining my feelings – if I could feel them – and making something out of them." When antidepressants are given to those in mourning, the symptoms may abate, though this does not provide a ticket to automatically feeling good. In most cases, the emotions of anguish and pain dissipate with enough time to process them. The process requires acknowledging the depth of despair associated with the loss, identifying the triggers of the feelings, then sharing them with someone close. This allows the sadness to shift, then lift as integration happens at conscious and unconscious levels. The process takes time, more than most people in contemporary society are willing to allocate or accommodate. Therefore, sadness is seen as a problem to be rid of rather than understood and supported.

Unhealthy and problematic sadness, depression, and anxiety occur when feeling responses are exaggerated, become unrealistic, or significantly inhibit day-to-day movement through the world. Symptoms should be monitored, and if they are persistent and non-remittent, evaluated by an objective mental health practitioner who can listen to behavioral syndromes in the social and psychological context of their occurrence.

Anxiety feels like a desperate need for action. When anxious, the autonomic nervous system works overtime and eventually causes the brain's communication system to work ineffectively. The thinking area of the brain becomes unable to balance and stay in sync with the emotional brain, resulting in an overload of fear producing messages. Unhealthy anxiety is measured when this fear response is out of proportion to the actual danger present. Typical symptoms of anxiety and grief include:

- Inability to relax
- Inability to sleep, or sleep comes in fitful episodes
- Feelings of fear without a reason
- Sense of generalized panic, losing control, or going "crazy"
- Difficulty concentrating
- Uncontrolled worries or ruminations that don't stop
- Irritability
- Fears of embarrassment in the presence of others

Depression is marked by the experience of five or more symptoms for at least two weeks without any sense of relief. The symptoms include:

- Depressed mood all of the time
- Lack of pleasure in all, or almost all, activities
- Significant weight loss or weight gain
- Insomnia
- Severe agitation or slowing down of typical day-to-day activities
- Extreme fatigue or loss of energy
- Feelings of worthlessness
- Diminished ability to think or concentrate
- Recurrent thoughts of death or suicide

No specific medications exist to treat the symptoms of grief. The use of medication depends heavily on the need of the patient and the advice provided by the mental health practitioner. Those with severe or complicated grief may benefit from antidepressant medications that lighten the weight of emotionality and keep debilitating thoughts at bay. Sleep medications may be helpful, too, but must be highly customized to individual need. While medications themselves cannot cure grief, they may be able to help the grieving person feel well enough to participate in other forms of therapy, which can provide real and lasting help.

SUPPORT GROUPS

Over the last few decades, it has become clear that the old view of grief as private has been replaced with an understanding of the importance of social connection in the grieving process. The research is conclusive: Positive social interactions are an important resource for coping with bereavement (Vachon & Stylianos, 1988). Much of the study has focused on the role of social support in assisting the bereaved though grief in the context of support groups. A mutual self-help group is defined as a cohort of people sharing a similar problem, who meet regularly to exchange information and to give and receive psychological support (Chinman, et al., 2002). Mutual help groups draw on the potential benefits of socially supportive interactions, utilizing the support from people who have gone through similar difficulties. This type of peer support is designed to compensate for deficiencies and gaps in an individual's natural support network. These types of groups are run principally by the members themselves and traditionally meet face to face, though grief groups typically have skilled facilitators holding an objective perspective and an established knowledge base that can handle mental issues and deal with any negative support or adverse events that may arise.

Many bereaved individuals have difficulty balancing the "paradox of letting go and remaining involved" (Klass, Silverman & Nickman, 1996) in relation to the loved one. After the death, most find that they need to discuss their feelings of loss with their informal support network, i.e., family and friends. Difficulties often arise, however, between the bereaved and this network. Families and friends feel anxious and awkward when faced with someone who is grieving. Advice may be unhelpful and occasionally hurtful. Friction can erupt in families when members cope differently, or when members feel their coping styles are criticized. Some family and friends create or maintain distance and silence, as one woman said, "because I just don't ever know what to say." Truthfully, it is easier to provide support to the bereaved who are perceived as coping well than to those who seem to flounder and remain lost in grief.

Support groups provide a place to talk about death, legitimize feelings, learn about the importance of ritual giving language and form to the paradox and obtain emotional support. Group members identify with others, and allow themselves to be helped through the reciprocal relationships created in the group. Support groups are known to be useful for receiving transitional support, since group support ultimately wanes as the individual integrates the loss (Parkes, 1998). Though there are many types and varieties of grief groups, their value in bereavement counseling and therapy is to provide general support that offers human comfort, care, and that accepts and encourages appropriate grief and mourning. These types of groups are typically interactive and educational.

While acknowledging that support groups are valuable for a grieving individual, there is a fair amount of data reporting low utilization and attendance in such grief groups, particularly given the number and type of offerings and extensive publicity. Attendance varies widely according to age of participants, group location, homogeneity of the community, and relationship of the bereaved with the agency providing the group. Those who attend support groups: "...hope for normalization, validation, healing, community, and opportunity for sharing. They want an opportunity to mourn with others in similar situations; they feel they need education on the grief process. Some bereaved are encouraged to attend by others, mainly adult children" (Steiner, 2006, p. 40). Those who choose not to attend generally report having enough overall support, a fear of loss of privacy, or for logistical reasons, such as time constraints or lack of transportation. One fellow said, "I just didn't want to feel vulnerable anymore. I don't want any more signs of weakness. I should be able to cope with this by myself."

The development, organization, and maintenance of a bereavement support groups is beyond the scope of this book. It is worthy, however, to note that those who do attend such groups want to feel better, gain hope, connect to others, and be well heard. Professionals leading support groups report that members initially perceive themselves as having limited support. As reported by the social worker Carol Steiner,

> Support groups seem very helpful in guiding many bereaved to become more realistic and accepting of their grief process. Groups help the bereaved receive emotional support, validation, education about grief and themselves, and coping techniques. They can gain a sense of control by being proactive. They gain different things from different groups at different points in their grief journey. They

are afforded opportunities to integrate their loss with their faith, to laugh without feeling guilty, and to have time for themselves away from family responsibilities. Finally, they are helped in remembering their loved one and provided with materials they can keep and use to help others. (2006, p. 41)

Anticipatory Grief

There is another facet of typical and expected grief to be considered, that of anticipatory grief. As has been discussed, typical uncomplicated grief and mourning occurs when an individual has died. When a loved one is diagnosed and treated with a serious illness, then moves toward end-of-life, a psychological response known as anticipatory grief manifests. This occurs when there is an expectation of death. It has many of the same signs and responses as those experienced after a death has happened. Anticipatory grief includes all of the thinking, feeling, cultural, and social reactions felt by the patient and family to an expected death. The watchword of anticipatory grief is angst: The loss becomes figural, and fear of the loss becomes more pronounced than actual grief.

Anticipatory grief includes feelings of sadness, depression, extreme concern for the dying person, preparing for the death, and adjusting to changes that will be caused by the loss of role functioning of the one who will die. One man described it as "many little deaths." This period of grief allows for intimates to begin acclimating to the reality of the loss, and opens a metaphorical window allowing for completion of unfinished business. Many people mistakenly believe that, by suffering anticipatory grief experienced before the death, actual post-death grief and hurt will be lessened. This is erroneous, as the grief process following the death has different trajectories, even if a survivor has suffered mightily with anticipatory grief.

There is discussion and debate whether or not anticipatory grief can be separated from the stresses of care giving for another who is at the end of life. Sufficient clinical evidence exists to suggest that anticipatory grief is a common occurrence, even though it may not happen with each caregiver. This grief response provides a bit of a safeguard for those close to the dying person and makes room for the stress of end-of-life care. The care giving research documents the challenges of attending to end-of-life issues and concerns. Many difficult and harsh emotions are prone to arise as the dying person lingers, including symptoms of burnout, feelings of isolation and disenfranchisement, resentment, and guilt at the progressive futility of care.

Grief counselors and therapists can offer great service to those caregivers dealing with anticipatory grief and compassion fatigue. Creation of a holding environment, safe enough for expression of what most feel should be unspoken, builds psychological space and offers the griever a sense of sanctuary in the midst of an ongoing storm.

V

Complications of Grief

To spare oneself from grief at all cost can be achieved only at the price of total detachment, which excludes the ability to experience happiness.

Erich Fromm

Grief teaches the steadiest minds to waver.

Sophocles

Close personal relationships enrich and undergird people's lives. Intimate relationships serve to regulate body and mind, and contribute to an overall sense of well-being (Sbarra & Hazan, 2008). Losing a close, strongly attached person is a profoundly painful and difficult experience. The experience of loss of this kind is associated with excessive risk of mortality and with decrements in both physical and mental health (van der Houwen, Stroebe, Stroebe, et al., 2010).

It is well known that no two people experience grief in the same way. Grief and healing are finely tuned to loss in a pattern and course unique to each person and relationship, with movement noted to occur in erratic and unpredictable ways. In general, though, over a period of months there is expected and discernible progress toward coming to terms with the loss. Eventually, most people "come to themselves," although there may be significant changes in beliefs and attitudes held before the death. In Western society, this is a false sense of closure and rarely happens quickly enough to satisfy the social network of the one who mourns. The 21st century lives by the motto of "Do more, do it better, with less, and do it faster." This is a troubling expectation that within a few days or weeks the bereaved should "get back into the swing of things." Typically, a long process of change lies ahead. Even though an individual may appear to have returned to baseline, "what looks like recovery to an observer may not feel like recovery to the bereaved person" (Rosenblatt, 2008, p. 9).

RISK FACTORS

A good body of research has been conducted on the risk factors associated with grief and bereavement. In general, those who are emotionally lonely and have an anxious attachment style to others are at greater risk for adversity. Those people taking psychotropic medication for anxiety, mood, or sleep problems are noted to experience more depressive and grief related symptoms than those who do not take such medicines. Loss of and lack of money are also associated with poor bereavement outcome. These markers make sense in their relation to grief, as they are secondary losses that add to the salience of the primary loss. It is unclear why people who experience financial deterioration also experience more loneliness. However, to counter the sense of loneliness and isolation, spirituality has been associated with a positive mood. Furthermore, the amount of perceived social support also predicts and neutralizes the intensity of grief and depressive symptoms, and increases the likelihood of positive mood.

The terms "grief" and "closure" are incompatible. Grief is not completed or resolved, but transformed through integration and a making of peace with the finality and consequences of the death. As bereavement proceeds, the mourner progressively re-visions the future in a way that once again has the possibility of joy and satisfaction. Memories of the deceased remain accessible, though bittersweet, and over time, the acute period of grief, where thoughts or images of the deceased painfully dominate the psychological landscape, eventually subsides.

ACUTE GRIEF

Acute grief is painful and disruptive, resembling a mental disorder. However, acute grief is not an illness and should not be labeled as one. The dominant emotion after the loss of a loved one is sadness combined with other emotions such as anger. The main function of typical grief is resignation, finally leading to adjustment with the new situation and circumstances of life. However, in addition to being a natural life event, it is a severe stressor and can trigger the onset of physical and psychological problems. At best, the healing process of grief is often difficult and contains traps that can hinder an individual's recovery. At worst, grief can accompany the onset or exacerbation of a mental disorder, which can derail natural healing. When the natural processes of grief and bereavement are compromised, differential considerations for care and resolution must be considered.

COMPLICATED GRIEF

For a distinct subset of grieving individuals, feelings of loss are continually debilitating and do not improve even after time passes. Complicated grief is an intense and long-lasting form of grief that takes over the survivor's life. Complicated grief is a form taking hold of the mind and that simply will not let go. In fact, one of the markers of complicated grief is the feeling of being stuck.

It has been noted for most people that as the loss is integrated, grief recedes into the background and healing diminishes the pain. Thoughts and memories become interwoven with lived experience, which warms the worldview of the survivor. While the absence of the physical presence of the deceased remains figural, the loss does not disrupt nor interrupt day to day living unless complicated grief comes into play. For those suffering with complicated grief, the pain of the loss becomes increasingly relevant and dominates the day, rather than receding into the background. Feelings of disbelief, loss, anguish, and bitterness permeate experience. There is an ongoing, intense distress related to separation, coupled with a strong yearning for the deceased. Such emotional overload comprises a number of cognitive, emotional, and behavioral factors.

This "complication" of grief interferes with the natural healing process. There are varieties of presentations of complicated grief. The benchmark symptom is marked by a difficulty to function effectively, including losing the capacity to care about recovery. William Worden proposed an early taxonomy to arrive at a conclusive definition of complicated grief. In 1991, he provided an operational definition for the construct and generated the following list of items:

- Abnormally short grief reaction
- Excessive and intense grief reaction
- Previous unresolved loss intruding on current grief
- Insufficient grief reaction
- Absence of satisfactory conclusion
- Excessive duration of grief reaction

- Maladaptive behavior
- Somatic or psychiatric symptoms
- Prolonged time before grief onset

People with complicated grief know their loved one is gone, but defensively deny or reject it. As one-woman said, "Time is moving on but I am not." These individuals often report strong feelings of yearning or longing for the person who died that do not seem to lessen over time or with repeated exposure to the gaps left by the loss. Thoughts, memories, or images ruminate and capture attention. Over time, there is an emergence of bitterness or anger related to the death. Another man said, "I can't imagine life without [my wife] to ever have purpose or meaning again. Joy and satisfaction are gone forever." Complicated grief often disrupts living relationships with friends and family members in the support system, which makes the bereaved individual feel increasingly cut off and alone.

Acute grief resembles a mental disorder and, while painful and disruptive, is a normative developmental process and not pathological. However, all forms of grieving are significant life stressors and can easily trigger the onset of physical and psychological health problems. The healing process is often difficult and complicated by traps that can ensnare the bereaved in ways that impair and impede progress toward integration of the loss.

To Diagnose or Not

Clinicians are familiar with the Diagnostic and Statistical Manual™ (DSM), which serves as the pre-eminent communication tool and professional shorthand for multi-disciplinary professionals. The original DSM was first published in 1952, with contemporary iterations dating from 1980, when a new rubric was fashioned, defining mental health disorders from a set of clearly drawn diagnostic criteria and accompanied by text providing additional behavioral information about each disorder. The text includes associated clinical features of the disorder, prevalence and familial patterns, differences in symptom presentation, culture and gender variations, and prognostic indicators. Since 1980, the DSM has had progressively higher degrees of validity and reliability in regard to diagnosis with each edition, and has yielded benchmark information regarding a disorder's likely course.

The fifth edition of the DSM has been published in 2013. Work groups researched and discussed revisions, inclusions, and exclusions for the new edition for six years. One of the fundamental changes to the DSM 5 is a shift in the features and considerations in the description of a mental disorder. The term *mental disorder* is defined as:

- A psychological syndrome or pattern of symptoms related to psychobiological dysfunction that causes clinically significant distress or impairment in functioning and is not an expectable response to a common stressor such as grief after loss, or a culturally appropriate response to an event such as a religious ritual.
- For each disorder, there are diagnostic validators such as prognostic significance, specific psychobiological change, specificity of response to treatments that differentiate a disorder from its "nearest neighbor." Each definition clinical utility, such as leading to better understanding, assessment, and treatment.
- When adding or deleting a diagnosis, potential benefits, such as better patient care or stimulating new research, should outweigh anticipated harms such as being subject to misuse (Shear, 2011, p. 103).

There has been great debate concerning the inclusion of a new diagnostic category that would define complicated grief as a diagnosable mental disorder. The working group provisionally placed the condition in the manual, calling it "bereavement-related disorder," and included it as a subtype of adjustment disorder. This caused multiple problems, particularly related to its temporal presentation and remission. The work group proposed that the addition be called adjustment disorder related to bereavement. The disorder was defined as present when "Following the death of a close family member or close friend, the individual experiences on more days than not intense yearning or longing for the deceased, intense sorrow and emotional pain, or preoccupation with the deceased or circumstances of the death for at least 12 months (or six months in children)." The criteria also described that "the person may also experience difficulty accepting the death, intense anger over the loss, a diminished sense of self, a feeling that life is empty, or difficulty planning for the future or engaging activities or relationships" (APA, 2012a). Criteria for another subtype, persistent complex bereavement-related disorder, were proposed for the section of the manual where conditions requiring further research would be placed. To meet the criteria for this disorder, symptoms should cause "marked distress that is in excess of what would be proportionate to the stressor" and/ or "significant impairment in social, occupational, or other important areas of functioning" (APA, 2012a). Through the different iterations considered by the various work groups, consensus was reached on several factors. The loss of a loved person should lead to significant separation distress that impairs social, occupational, and other important areas of functioning. There should be an identifiable constellation of cognitive, emotional, and behavioral symptoms that impair reconciliation and meaning attribution.

Since the publication of the DSM-III in 1980, recent bereavement was seen as an exclusion criterion for the diagnosis of a major depressive disorder. Inclusion and exclusion criteria were reconsidered, as well for DSM 5. The exclusion criterion in the DSM-IV applied to people experiencing depressive symptoms lasting less than two months following the death of a loved one. The Mood Disorder Work Group then removed the bereavement exclusion from the DSM 5. It was replaced by several notes within the text delineating the differences between grief and depression, reflecting the recognition that bereavement is a severe psychosocial stressor that can precipitate a major depressive episode beginning soon after the loss of a loved one. As the work group stated, "The preponderance of data suggest that bereavement-related depression is not different from a major depressive episode that presents in any other context; it is equally genetically influenced, most likely to occur in individuals with past personal and family histories of major depressive episodes, has similar personality characteristics and patterns of comorbidity, is as likely to be chronic and/or recurrent, and responds to antidepressant medications" (Zisook, Corruble, Duan, et al., 2012, p. 425).

Regardless of the diagnostic nosology, complicated grief can be debilitating. Relentless and prominently troubling thoughts related to the death or its aftermath, persistent and unregulated emotions, and excessive avoidance or compulsive proximity-seeking to "things" of the deceased that complicate daily functioning can derail an accepted and uncomplicated grieving process. Rumination over concerns of the circumstances of the loss, difficulty making sense of the world, catastrophic misinterpretation of the consequences of actions, or excessive avoidance of reminders of the death are also constellations of symptoms found in those experiencing complicated grief. Overall, there is a sense of "stuckness" in the revolving round of symptom presentation. Emotions, thoughts, coping, and general health feel compromised. Research suggests that complicated grief occurs in about 10-20% of bereaved individuals, varying widely upon the circumstances of death (Middleton, Burnett, Raphael, & Martinek, 1996).

Depending on the espoused school of counseling theory and interpretation of empirical data, there are varying opinions about what objectively defines complicated grief. There is sufficient data to report about the factors that increase the risk of complicated grief, including:

- An unexpected or violent death
- Suicide of a loved one
- Lack of support system or friendships
- Early history of child abuse or neglect
- Childhood separation anxiety
- Overly dependent relationship with the deceased
- Lack of preparation for the death
- Poor coping skills, adaptive functioning, and low resilience

Most scholars and clinicians agree that complicated grief does not emerge until a minimum of six months have passed since the death. The grieving individual then experiences a constellation of symptoms including:

- Strong feelings of yearning or longing for the person who died
- Feelings of intense loneliness, even when others are around and wish to be supportive
- Strong feelings of anger or bitterness related to the death
- Existential emptiness or loss of meaning without the person who died
- Obsessions or ruminations to the extent that they disrupt daily life
- Strong feelings of disbelief about the death or difficulty accepting the death as time passes
- Increasing feelings of shock or emotional numbing
- Loss of ability to care about or trust others
- Physical or emotional agitation in the presence of reminders of the loss
- Avoidance of people, places, or things that are reminders of the loss
- Strong urges to see, touch, hear, or smell things to feel close to the one who has died

Treatment for complicated grief seems to follow familiar strategies and interventions for depression, anxiety, and trauma. Best treatment practices have yet to be empirically validated. In general, therapy seeks to help the client explore and process emotions, improve coping skills, and reduce feelings of blame and guilt. Complicated grief is relatively unresponsive to antidepressants

(Pasternak, Reynolds, Schlerntzuaer, Hoch, Buysse, et al., 1991) and seems to respond well to a mix of interpersonal and cognitive-behavior therapies (similar to PTSD-targeted psychotherapy). General therapy goals include exploration of unconscious panic and distress while increasing coping and adaptive strategies and skills. Individuals suffering from complicated grief are helped to stabilize, explore, and confront the most painful aspects of the loss, then finally to integrate and transform their grief.

Ambiguous Loss

The researcher Pauline Boss (1999) has coined the term *ambiguous loss* for a particular complication of grief marked by a lack of resolution of the loss which she calls "frozen sadness." An ambiguous loss remains unclear and indeterminate, leaving the grieving individual in an uncertain state of emotional suspended animation. As Boss says, "Here we see the absurdity of not being certain about a person's absence or presence. People hunger for certainty. Even sure knowledge of death is more welcome than a continuation of doubt" (1999, p. 6).

There are two basic kinds of ambiguous loss. In the first type, a person is perceived by family members/support system as physically absent but psychologically present, because it is unclear whether they are dead or alive, e.g., soldiers missing-in-action or kidnapped children. A more everyday occurrence includes loss due to divorce, where a parent is viewed as absent or missing. The second type finds a person perceived as physically present but psychologically absent, e.g., an individual living with Alzheimer's disease. In both types of loss, those who grieve have to deal with extraordinary loss. There is an inability to resolve the loss due to the external situation, rather than only as an internal process related to attachment. The outside forces related to the loss freeze grief in uncertainty. An ambiguous loss never allows those who grieve the detachment necessary for full integration. In truth, people in the presence of an ambiguous loss cannot begin to grieve because the situation is indeterminate. What feels like a loss is not really one. Therefore, the confusion freezes and suspends what would otherwise be an uncomplicated grieving process. Boss frames this process as 'leaving without goodbye/goodbye without leaving.'

The experience of ambiguous loss leaves people filled with conflicting thoughts and feelings. The tension that results from conflicting emotions tends to become overwhelming. Individuals have progressive difficulty with decisions, actions, and letting-go. Ambiguous loss is characterized by ambivalence, which is psychologically understood "…to indicate a conflict between positive and negative feelings toward a person or set of ideas" (Boss, 1999, p. 61). From this definition, ambivalence is noted to be an internal process. Its internal state can be amplified and intensified by deficiencies in the environment. This pulls the individual in opposing directions, binding and restricting clear thinking, feeling, or plans for action. Ambiguous loss tends to blur tidy boundaries. While traditional approaches of counseling and therapy for the resolution of ambivalent feelings hinges on recognition of the two opposing sides of feeling, the external situation must be addressed to effectively meet the demands of ambiguous loss. Until the ambiguity is resolved and clarified, the tension remains. For practitioners, ambiguous loss should be validated and labeled as being responsible for the conflicting feelings. As Boss writes, "Knowing that under such circumstances mixed feelings are normal, and knowing the situation is not their fault, people are less resistant to therapy or interventions aimed at helping them recognize the full range of their feelings" (Boss, 1999, p. 76).

SUICIDE AND ITS AFTERMATH

Death by suicide affects not only the person committing suicide but many others as well. It is estimated that for every suicide there are six survivors in the deceased's intimate system. Suicide is an irreversible act, which often arises from stressors that could have been alleviated with help or simply by allowing time to pass. It is generally viewed as a sudden and unexpected act. Regrettably, the ability to clinically predict suicide with any degree of accuracy is limited. Despite vast literature on the subject, there is no gold standard nor a single test or method of assessment that identifies the individual who will complete suicide. Therefore, descriptions of suicide epidemiology are more relevant for practitioners who will help the survivors of such a tragic loss.

Suicide is currently the ninth leading cause of death in the United States, with firearms accounting for around two-thirds of completed suicides. Nearly three quarters of all completed suicides are committed by Caucasian males; with the highest completion rate in this group are men over the age of 85. Suicide is the third leading cause of death among young people aged 15 to 24 (following unintentional injuries and homicide). About 12 in every 100,000 young people in this age group will complete suicide (American Association of Suicidology, 2005). Overall, this translates to around 90 completed suicides per day in the United States.

Depending upon the source, there are an estimated eight to 25 attempted suicides to one completion. The ratio of attempts to completions is higher in women and youth and lower in men and the elderly (although, as noted above, men are more prone to complete). More women than men report a history of attempted suicide, with a gender ratio of about two to one. The strongest risk factors for attempted suicide in adults are depression, alcohol abuse, cocaine use, and separation or divorce. The strongest risk factors for attempted suicide in youth are depression, alcohol or other substance use disorders, and aggressive or disruptive behavior problems.

Clearly, prevention is key for the suicidal individual. While outside of the scope of this book, preventive strategies and research are worthy when considering interventions related to a suicidal person and the surviving support system. Because suicide and its aftermath is a constellation of highly complex behaviors, preventive interventions must also be complex and intensive if they are to have lasting effects over time. Based on reliable findings from the research literature, recognition and appropriate treatment of mental and substance abuse disorders is the most promising way to prevent suicide and suicidal behavior in all age groups. Most elderly suicidal individuals will have visited their primary care physician in the month prior to the event. There is growing evidence that training primary care providers to recognize and treat depressive episodes is a promising way to prevent suicide among the elderly. Among young people, limiting access to firearms and promoting responsible firearms ownership, especially in conjunction with the treatment of mental and addictive disorders, seems to be the most beneficial avenues for preventing suicide by firearm. Regrettably, the common sense approach of school-based, information only prevention programs, focused solely on suicide, have not been evaluated for their efficacy. These "information only" programs can increase the distress in young people who are the most vulnerable. Current thinking orients to the examination of school and community programs. As a broader focus of mental health, such programs target substance abuse and disruptive behavior disorders and teach coping skills in response to stress. These programs are more successful in the long run.

For members of the suicide completer's intimate and social system, life after suicide is complicated. Survivors show more feelings of rejection and higher levels of anger toward the deceased than survivors of those who have died in other ways (Barrett and Scott, 1990). They have been shown to exhibit severe feelings of guilt and responsibility for the death, experience high levels of shame and stigma, and struggle with finding explanations and meaning around the suicide (Silverman, Range, and Overholser, 1995).

Most researchers studying suicide report that this type of loss does not heal. The effects may stabilize, but the loss stays electric and painful. Bereaved individuals and families are typically referred to SOS (Survivors of Suicide) support groups. Many suicide survivors will approach such group work with skepticism, particularly if the deceased had been in any kind of counseling or therapy at the time of the suicide. However, the primary benefits of mutual self-help allow those living with the loss to be reassured that others share similar fears and losses, and that there is no pathology associated with the post traumatic feelings related to the suicide. Such groups serve as a conduit for organizing and understanding thoughts and feelings. Peer support groups provide healthy role models from others in different developmental stages of addressing the loss.

In a larger community, the topic of suicide is defined by its silence. When a suicide occurs, it is quickly hidden and wrapped in denial and shame. The community is prone to edit use of the word 'suicide' in funeral rites, rituals, and conversations. Discussing the circumstances of this kind of death is socially taboo, and spoken in hushed terms, if at all. Such stigmatization is especially painful for survivors, who may already be feeling guilt and culpability for their loved one's death. As one woman said, following her teenage son's completed suicide, "I keep trying to make sense out of his death, but there is just nothing rational. I still cannot figure out what I did to contribute to this, but I know it is easier to tolerate my own failings than it is to accept that someone I loved died by his own will."

DISENFRANCHISED GRIEF

The concept of disenfranchised grief comes from the work of Kenneth Doka (2002) and is defined as grief that persons experience when they incur a loss that is not or cannot openly be acknowledged, socially sanctioned, or publically mourned. The concept integrates psychological and sociological perspectives on grief and loss. An individual may have an intensely personal experience of loss, but that loss may not be validated by society, family, or friends.

A fellow described the death of his best friend. "We had been friends for over thirty years. We started being buddies in elementary school. Both of us went away to college, got married, raised families, and stayed in close touch throughout all time. We saw each other fairly frequently, mostly coming back to the rural town where we were raised. We celebrated life events with each other and our families. Then he had what they called a widow maker heart attack. He was alive one minute and dead the next. We went through the funeral, comforted his family and they comforted me, and I went home. No one here knows much, other than I had a close friend who died. I'm embarrassed to say how much I miss him, and there really is no place to take my grief. I go to write an email, to pick up the phone, and there's nothing that I can do except shudder. I am staying in contact with his wife and grown children, but I feel out of place with them. After all, he was her husband and the kids' father. I was just his friend."

Like this gentlemen, individuals in this situation are not offered rights to the grieving role, such as a claim to social sympathy and support, or such compensations as time off from work or a lessening of social responsibilities. There are conflicts for disenfranchised grievers with informal cultural expectations about how grief can be expressed. Without the cultural and external validation, the individual grieves the loss with a particular type of psychic pain. Even though the man in the example describes the deceased in many ways as a brother, the relationship is not recognized or based on kinship ties. Therefore, there is no public permission to grieve the loss. The loss for the bereaved is not defined as socially significant. In fact, as the man in the example said, "No one here knows much, except I had a close friend who died." This leaves the mourner feeling on the outside of what is socially appropriate and expected in mourning rights and rituals.

Disenfranchised grief is most often times managed in private because of limited access to socially relevant resources. It is hidden grief, though it takes the same course as any other process of reconciling and integrating loss. To help another move through disenfranchised grief, the loss must be fully recognized as real, and genuine time must be given to grieve. Because of the nature of disenfranchised grief, professional counseling and therapy is recommended to allow full voice to the griever.

VI

Grief and the Impact of Death on the Family

And if I go, whilst you're still here…know that I live on, vibrating to a different measure behind a thin veil….

Emily Dickenson

So long as we live they too shall live and love for they are a part of us, as we remember them.

Gates of Prayer

FAMILY SYSTEMS PERSPECTIVE

The concept of a system is used to refer to a group of people who interact as a functional whole. Neither people nor their problems exist in a vacuum, but are inextricably interwoven within broader interactional systems, the most fundamental being the family. The family is the primary agent for transmitting a worldview from generation to generation, which has been described as an organizing structure for what happens in the wider world (Hiebert, 2009).

The family is the primary, and except in rare instances, the most powerful system to which a person ever belongs. The typical family is defined by the entire kinship network of three generations, both as it currently exists and as it has evolved through time. The physical, social, and emotional functioning of family members are profoundly interdependent, with changes in one part of the system reverberating through other parts of the system. Families' interactions and relationships have three organizing properties – they are reciprocal, patterned, and repetitive. The reciprocity of the system allows for mutual relationships to be interchangeable and move in correspondence with each other when the system is stressed. Change is not seen as being caused by a triggering event but in the interplay of responses that are governed by the structure of the family's relationships. By definition, the family is required to balance a sense of change with a sense of continuity; it works to stabilize itself in habitual and rhythmic mechanisms. The patterning of the family defines its personality, allowing subsequent generations to understand the system's model of functioning. Finally, families repeat themselves. The repetitive and redundant nature of a family allows for tentative predictions to be made, based on the family's history. The same issues tend to be played out from one generation to the next, even though the actual behavior may take a variety of forms. Children learn the way the world works from previous generations. The home is the first setting for looking at self, others, and the world. As children grow, make friendships, and meet partners, their worldview expands and diffuses. Families build these unique meaning structures that guide them to experience, interpret, and track their lives as individuals and as a family.

When considering the dynamics of life and loss, a developmental approach to family bereavement seems particularly applicable. The family's worldview and grief experience come together in narratives and stories about the death. Viewing death as an expected piece of the ebb and flow of change over the family life cycle allows a benign stance to understanding the family as it faces the demands in its ordinary circumstances. Grief from a developmental perspective approaches death as a family transition involving crises of attachment identity for individual family members; these must be incorporated into the ongoing flow of the family's lifespan. If family members perceive consistency in the life and relationships held with the deceased, there is generally more of a sense of unity of grief that is flexible enough to assimilate information about death without shattering its foundation. The natural balance of the family requires management of intense emotionality and the redirection of the course of the family's development. The discontinuity of death causes the family to struggle to absorb and reintegrate the loss. Such a re-establishment of balance is needed to restore the family's flow of developmental time and place with preferred patterns of communication, relating in social role functioning, and integrating the death experience in the family's narrative of shared meaning. The prime developmental task revolves around the homeostatic balance of change and stability.

The process of restoring family equilibrium in order to tolerate the disruptive implications of death requires systemic resources and the creation of new self-organizing structures for the family (Shapiro, 1994, p. 49). These resources for instituting new stable structures include:

1. Private individual processes for managing intense emotions and making sense of an overwhelming experience
2. Family system strategies for shared stabilization under circumstances of overwhelming stress
3. Extended family and community supports for managing day-to-day living and interpreting the meaning of the death and loss
4. Cultural rituals interpreting the death and its meanings and prescribing roles for the survivors.

The rhythms of the family's approach to loss will vary with the degree of stress and discontinuity in the circumstances of the death, the available support needed to balance the distress, the nature of the family's developmental history, and the availability of cultural rituals and grief practices. The greater the family's degree of stress and discontinuity prior to the death, the greater the family's risk for diminished integrity in the presence of the loss. Families with a high degree of premorbid stress are prone to dissociate and distance from the overwhelming aspects of the grief experience, and will, paradoxically, work to restrict the developmental tasks of accommodating to the loss. Bereavement is unconsciously viewed as a state of disequilibrium, rather than a natural approach to balance.

Families typically respond to the death of a loved one with systemic "craziness," defined as a normal response to an abnormal situation. Family members report psychosocial disruption and psychic pain as the loss of certainty of life, an increased sense of helplessness, the loss of a right to feel angry or feel what are typically defined as "negative" emotions directed toward the deceased, the loss of an ability to care for the self without experiencing guilt, and confusion regarding shifting role functions within the family system. An overarching task for the grieving family revolves around the shared acknowledgement of the reality of the death and the loss of the family member. The obvious change is found in the physical absence of the deceased, with the less obvious, though equally potent loss of the deceased's role functions and the need to reallocate those tasks to surviving family members. Shared experience of the pain of grief and the loss, coupled with reorganization of the family system and redirection of the family's relationships and goals, can create undue stress as the family seeks a new rhythm following the death.

Typically, there is a high degree of systemic confusion. Such confusion is closely related to information-seeking and the corresponding anxiety of what is necessary to "know" in order to proceed to the next step. Prioritization and limit-setting becomes pivotal for rebalancing the system. Because death is typically a new experience for most families, a validation of the system's needs helps underline and delegate the tasks related to meeting the experienced demands placed on the system. When a family member dies, the person leaves empty roles and severed relationships. The nature of grief experienced by the survivors reflects the type of relationship ended by death. This loss creates a need for the family to make certain that the important role functions are addressed. An informal network will emerge until there is some sense that the role can be re-allocated. The instability of the family is usually transitory as roles shift and change.

DEATH OF A CHILD

The death of a child is incomprehensible and devastating. Such a loss disrupts the lives of those affected for many years after the actual event. In Western society, the death of a child has generally been found to elicit more intense and complicated grief reactions than other types of bereavement (Sanders, 1989). Such a death places a parent and siblings at heightened risk of psychological suffering and decrements in functioning. Compared to losing other loved ones, the death of a child is inherently out of sync with the family life cycle and violates the perceived order of natural living. As researchers Joan Arnold and Penelope Gemma (2008) write, "The associated lifelong grief for parents becomes the connection between parent and child beyond the child's death. As parents grieve their child, the breadth and depth of loss are enfolded into their lives, defining a new identity shaped by grieving. Grief unfolds as the parent lives with loss, without the dead child, and in a new and transformed reality" (p. 658). Although the majority of bereaved parents and families find ways to resume productive lives, there is evidence showing that grief symptoms for parents who outlive their children frequently endure throughout the life span.

Parental and family grief resulting from the death of a child is profound regardless of the years since death, the age of the child at the time of death, and the cause of the death of the child. "Insofar as a child's development largely depends on the quality of the attachment relationship with his or her parents, being a parent is an underestimated developmental achievement for many persons that can engender a sense of identity and purpose. Therefore, when a child dies, many parents not only experience sadness over losing a valued member of the family; they feel that a part of themselves has somehow died as well" (Malkinson & Bar-Tur, 2005, p. 104). The nature of parental/ familial grief and its dimensions are well detailed in the clinical literature. Overall, grief related to the death of a child is felt as a deeply personal and unique experience. However, parents and siblings report they feel "joined" to other families who share a similar experience of loss. There are general phenomenological themes that emerge from the death of a child, according to Arnold and Gemma (2008), including:

- The grief is complex, and persists throughout the parent's life. Family history and experience provide perspective, but nothing prepares the parents/family for the death of their child.

- The family will find multiple ways to remain connected to the deceased, including using sensual cues, images, and rituals.

- Bereaved family members desire to share their grief, but find that few others will ask or willingly listen about the death of the child. Support varies and comes from expected and unexpected people and places.

- Faith systems matter in the grieving process, though there is no clear expectation as to whether spirituality will be strengthened or weakened.

- There will be corresponding secondary losses to the death of the child, e.g., marriage, support systems, work, which may be viewed favorably or unfavorably.

- Expressions of loss are always close to the surface, even after an extended amount of time has passed since the death.

- Relationships with surviving and subsequent children are strengthened. Parenting for the deceased child continues after the death through memory, remembrances, loving, and caring.

The intense and enduring symptoms of grief that parents and families report reflect the difficult challenge of integrating this seemingly incomprehensible loss into the fabric of meaning that gives the system an overarching sense of purpose, predictability, and order. There are several factors related to the context of the child's death to be considered in bereavement adaptation. The attachment relationship to the child, violence related to the death, and length of bereavement uniquely contribute to the intensity of related thoughts and feelings. Research suggests that mothers generally report more grief than fathers (though this may be under-reported). Surviving children may find that parents become anxious as they seek to reassure themselves about their remaining children. Parents and family members who are able to find a sense of understanding in the loss are known to have the most effective post-loss adjustment.

When a loss occurs in a child's life, whether it is sibling or friend, attempts are often made by well-meaning adults to minimize its effects. Such a course of action has limited usefulness, as death is a fact of life that comes to all – some sooner than later. The constructive approach to death is to help the surviving child explore personal feelings and develop an age appropriate understanding of it. Children are capable of experiencing grief and can experience similar physical and emotional symptoms as adults. Caregivers are reminded that children differ from adults, though, in their cognitive abilities, coping styles, need for identification figures, and dependence on adults for support. Children tend to be quite resilient, and adults who are careful to listen to the child's concerns will communicate support for well-being. A child's response to loss reflects the influence of age, stage of mental and emotional development, the patterns of interactions and communication within the family, the relationship with the person who died, and previous experiences with death. As with adults, deaths that are sudden and unexpected or that result from suicide or violence may complicate the issues that the child faces in coming to terms with the loss. Children will typically look to parental figures for help in understanding the death of a sibling or friend. The parents' method of coping is an important determinant of how the child copes. Children usually cope more easily with their feelings about a close death when they feel that they are included as participants in the unfolding experience. If they are excluded or their questions unanswered, uncertainty in the child's mind creates more anxiety, confusion, and pain. Children have natural curiosity, and will want information as they can sense any withholding.

Though an anguished process, reviewing, retelling, and reconstructing narratives of loss in a way that permits fuller integration of the experience of the child's death benefits those parents and family members who struggle with prolonged and intense grieving (Keesee, Currier, & Neimeyer, 2008).

DEATH OF AN ADULT

The patterns of coping with loss continue to evolve throughout a person's lifespan. Developmentally, all phases of life are connected, with each building on the one before. As is taught in Psychology 101, each developmental stage has a crisis associated with it. Successfully negotiating this developmental task gives maturational strength of wisdom and character, which the developmental psychologist Erik Erikson described as "informed and detached concern with life itself in the face of death itself" (1982, p. 67). Erikson's work was concerned with individual development. Regarding loss and the family's developmental structure, when an adult dies the "we-ness" of the family changes. Since this sense of "we" is created early in the family and is characteristic of the personality of the system, intense emotional experiences, including the death of one of its members, opens a window in the system to re-evaluate its capacities and functions in a normative developmental process.

Loss of a parent.   As an individual ages, the causes of death and the processes of dying change. While the death of a child is often sudden and unexpected, an adult death from disease or the aging process allows time to plan, consider, and anticipate the impact of death on the system. In this day and time as people are living longer, adults are faced with many opportunities to meet death. Parents are living to older age, and middle-aged adults become caregivers for their elders. While contemporary society offers no clearly defined roles for adult children of dying parents, each family develops its own ways of functioning. When death comes, depending on the nature of the relationship, the care giving provided, and reconciliation of unfinished business, members of the system have a wide variety of incorporation and integration strategies for the loss. Even if there is an anticipatory time associated with death, the loss has a profound effect on the family survivors. Among other changes, the death of a parent takes the adult child into the presence of mortality. The death of a parent is an important symbolic event for midlife adults. It seems to be a universal developmental "push" into greater maturity.

When a family relationship has been dysfunctional, the death of a parent brings an end to the hope of creating better, more functional relationships. As one fellow said as he attended to his elderly dying mother, "She was incredibly difficult to love. In fact, we used to say she was 'Hell-on-Wheels.' She had a stroke in her early 90s and then lingered. I always thought that this would be a place where I would want to see her. But it didn't happen that way. What I saw was a frail elder, completely dependent and helpless. It really made me stop and think. There was no use in holding onto old grudges. The things that had happened in the past just didn't matter any longer. My mother couldn't harm me, and I was a better man than to try and take advantage of her as she died. It was really regrettable that she didn't have more love around her at the end of her life, but that was something that I couldn't change. I could live with the regrets better than I could live with the anger, though. That gave me some peace. I really don't know if it provided her any ease, but I realized that I was there to provide compassionate care – something that I would've done for anyone in her situation." In this and similar incidents, the man realized that he had lost his symbolic "parent" and was caring for a dying human being. While he would certainly wish that it could have been different, his ability to be involved in his own process provided a sense of integration.

Loss of a spouse.   The loss of a spouse is the most intensely studied of all adult deaths. Most research has focused on married heterosexual couples. As there is greater social acceptance and political reform regarding gay long-term relationships, there will be new and complementary information available in the public discourse. The patterns of long-term partner or spousal loss may be carefully considered and broadened beyond a traditional heterosexual template, regardless of the social or political sanctions of such relationships. What is primary in considering the loss of a long-term partner are the patterns of intimacy and interaction between the spouses/partners. These patterns form the determinants of how the loss of a partner will be perceived by the survivors.

Bereaved spouses report depressive symptoms during the first year following the loss, though younger people seem to experience more physical distress and tend to rely more on psychopharmacology aides to counter the distress than older people do (DeSpelder & Strickland, 1999). That being said, older people may have health problems that are neglected while caring for an ailing partner. In the first year following the loss of a mate, there are increases in morbidity and mortality rates of all widows and widowers, with aged people at particular risk. Relief following the death of a spouse, particularly if there has been long-term care giving involved, is rarely discussed. Spousal bereavement elicits distinct behaviors related to culturally sanctioned gender roles, which vary from community to community.

Those couples who lived out traditional sex roles may find the transition following the loss of a partner particularly troublesome and difficult. Those widowed persons whose life styles include multiple roles seem to experience a better adjustment to bereavement than those with fewer role involvements. As one widow reported, "I had to become something other than 'wife.' That had been my primary role throughout my adult life. A big part of dealing with my grief was to become known as friend, alter guild member, library volunteer, Democrat activist – all things that defined me outside of what I was in my relationship with my deceased husband. I had to become more self-reliant, and this was not a way that I understood myself, nor did others – including my children – think that I could manage. I've surprised them. I've surprised myself."

CAREGIVING RISK

In 2005, the Centers for Disease Control reported that 70% of deaths in the United States were the result of chronic diseases such as cancer, heart disease, Alzheimer's, respiratory diseases, stroke, Parkinson's, and diabetes (CDC, 2005). Many of these chronic illnesses impact physical functioning. Because the United States does not have a well-defined formal care system for supporting those with chronic diseases, family members often take on care giving for an ill and dying individual. The intensity and kind of care provided by family members varies. While most caregivers are able to meet the demands of extraordinary care, there is a large body of literature that shows the negative impact of care giving before an ill person's death. Caregiving requires extraordinary effort, defined by a significant expenditure of time and energy, often for extended periods of time, requiring the performance of tasks that may be physically demanding and unpleasant, frequently disrupting the caregiver's other family and social roles. The demands of such care are usually associated with global physical, emotional, and time strains. Caregivers are more likely to be distressed when patients have more symptoms, greater loss of physical function, and more complicated needs.

The research base has focused on three theories regarding the emotional effects of bereavement after care giving. The first is referred to as resource depletion, which argues that emotional, physical, and economic stressors experienced during care giving deplete coping resources, which depletes the coping resources needed to meet the demands of grief. Caregivers often report the "wear and tear" of the process to be exhausting and one for which recovery is slow. The second is actually the opposite of the first and related to the relief, which predicts that the reduced responsibility and stress on the caregivers after the death improves physical and mental health. The third theory suggests that because death is more likely to be anticipated in the care giving context, much of the grief work occurs before the death.

After the death of a care recipient, family caregivers may experience many negative psychological outcomes, most of which revolve around depressive symptoms and syndromes. The location of care and of death appears to have an impact on the grief experience. Caregivers who reported that their care recipient had a higher fear of death, and those who said they had family members who had difficulty accepting the illness had higher senses of adverse effects than those without these experiences. The intensity of care provided seems to place the caregiver at risk for complications following the loss. Family caregivers of those with dementia were also found to fare worse than caregivers of people with other chronic conditions (Shuter, Edwards, & Sacre, 2008). The uncertain trajectory of dementia, the need for caregivers to make decisions that may conflict with those of the ill person, and witnessing the erosion of autonomy and independence contribute to the caregiver's distress after the death. Caregivers also report that feelings of exhaustion and having a high sense of burden during care giving, regardless of the care recipient's disease, are also associated with grief and that, as one caregiver succinctly said, "I should have done more." Those caregivers reporting this sense of burden report lower feelings of relief after the death and frequent negative thoughts about the care provided before the death. Interestingly, though, those caregivers who reported more benefit of care giving were also more likely to experience adverse symptoms of grief and bereavement. There may be two explanations for this: Losing a care recipient triggers feelings of deprivation for a meaningful and important role, or a positive view of care giving may indicate a high level of attachment or dependency between the caregiver and the person cared for.

There is interesting preliminary research that discusses negative interactions with professional providers as a risk for caregivers. As the United States healthcare system continues to devolve and fragment, caregivers are frequently asked to serve as more assertive advocates for their care recipient. Intuitively and supported in qualitative studies, feelings of being ignored or unsupported by professional healthcare providers, including end-of-life care providers, are predictors of complications for the grief of caregivers. As one caregiver reported, "I never had a sense that the physician was comforting. All I wanted for my mother was compassion and ordinary decency. We eventually had to put her in a nursing home, which did not provide me any relief at all. There were not enough aides to care for her, and as a general rule, they seemed to resent having to do any hands-on care. I know it may be crazy, but I expected that people would put aside their own beliefs and tend to what was most appropriate at the time to care for my mother. It just didn't happen this way. I began to believe that the philosophy of new medicine is 'a live patient is a paying patient.' Not too generous, I know, but the lack of a willingness to listen just wore me out."

A sense of preparedness about the death seems to buffer the impact of the loss. Even knowing that a relative is terminally ill, many caregivers and family members will say that the death was "unexpected" and they were left feeling unprepared and that the death came "too soon." However, knowing that a death is imminent is not the same as being prepared for it. Those caregivers at higher risk for adverse effects of grief seem to be spouses, younger women, those without much social support, and those who report the lack of being prepared for the death.

VII

The Social Ceremonies of Loss

I went to a funeral
Lord it made me happy
Seeing all those people
That I ain't seen
Since the last time
Somebody died
Everybody talking
They were telling funny stories
Saying all those things
That they ain't said
Since the last time
Somebody died

Lyle Lovett, "Since the Last Time"

The choice of last rites speaks to individual, familial, and community attitudes and beliefs about loss. The social ceremonies of loss are punctuation marks for the death of one of its members. Like a comma or period at the end of a sentence, last rites provide definition and demarcation of the way things have changed. What is enacted is an expression, through symbol and metaphor, of how death is perceived and understood within that particular group. Every social, cultural, and ethnic group has essential elements to underscore the passing of one of its members. Just as a community convenes to commemorate other major social transitions in a person's life, such as birth or marriage, the last rites provide an opportunity for survivors to gather together and remember the deceased's participation in the community and the member's passing and absence from the group. The communal acknowledgement of death serves social and psychological purposes to be discussed.

84

Habit, Tradition, and Ritual

Linguistically, a distinction is necessary to effectively discuss the social ceremonies of grief and loss. The terms habit, tradition, and ritual are often used interchangeably, though they have different trajectories and hold different meanings when considering death, grief, bereavement, and the mourning ceremonies associated with the process. The notion of habit and tradition will be discussed initially, with focus being placed on the value of ritual in the rites of passage and integration of loss through grief.

A *habit* is a routine of behavior that is repeated regularly and tends to occur automatically. Psychologists define a habit as a more or less fixed way of thinking, willing, or feeling acquired through repetitive mental experiences. Habitual behavior often goes unnoticed, because a person does not need to engage in self-analysis or observation when undertaking routine tasks. Acquiring a habit is an extremely simple form of learning: An organism, after a period of exposure to a stimulus, stops responding to that stimulus with varied behaviors and begins to respond in an automatic way. As behaviors are repeated in a consistent context, a link is formed between the context and the action, which increases the automatic performance of the behavior. Habits are useful in their efficiency. People do not have to pay attention to themselves to engage in habit-driven behavior. Because of the association of the behavior to the context, the habit occurs naturally and without consideration of control. Habits are personal and unique.

Traditions are basic beliefs and behaviors originating in the past that are passed down within a community or society defining its contemporary character. Traditions evolve and persist over time as they are taught by one generation to the next, then performed or believed in the present. The word 'tradition' is derived from the original Latin term *trader* which means to transmit, to hand over, and to give for safekeeping. While it is commonly assumed that traditions are ancient, unalterable, and deeply important, many customs are invented for a specific cultural purpose over a relatively short period of time. Sociologists generally presume that at least two transmissions over three generations are required for a practice or belief to be seen as traditional.

Family holiday traditions provide an example. One young woman told her story, saying, "When I got married, I upset the family tradition. My parents wanted us to come to their home for Christmas. As we had young children, we wanted to stay home and establish our own traditions. This change upset my family's sense of what was right and wrong. My mother said, 'we've always done it this way' and had a good deal of difficulty accepting that we wanted to establish our own ways of celebrating." The young woman's mother, in her ways of thinking and action, demonstrates a logical flaw often attributed to the understanding of traditions. The argument that takes the form of "this is right because we've always done it this way," can be refuted on the grounds that the "tradition" is no longer desirable, or may never have been despite its popularity. The newly established family wanted their own traditions.

Another woman told an elegant story illustrating this idea. "In my family, there was an old tradition of holding a long-gone elder's cut glass sugar bowl that was to be passed down to the next generation's oldest female member. Nobody ever knew how the custom started or why it continued. It was just a rite of passage and was like glue that held my family together, revered by all. I had received the sugar bowl years ago as the eldest of my generation and kept it in a high cabinet, safe and away from display."

"My oldest niece was to be married. As we were preparing for the wedding, I thought it would be a good time to pass the sugar bowl on to her. One afternoon I took it out of the cabinet to clean it, and it slipped out of my hand. It hit the counter and dropped on the floor, shattering into what looked like a thousand pieces. I could not believe it. I got on my knees and started picking up the pieces. Just as I got my first big 'boo-hoo' out, I took a deep breath and started laughing. I said to myself, 'Well, that's over with. Who knows what kind of baggage went with that old bowl anyway? The messages contained in that bowl held a whole lot more than sugar. I was surprised at the relief that I felt, even though it was a little sad for the tradition to end."

Traditions serve to highlight or enhance the importance of a social institution. They are subtly adapted over time to suit the needs of the day so that the changes can become accepted as a part of the history or ancient-ness of the "way it has always been." Traditions change slowly. As long as they are performed in context, changes from one generation to the next are not seen as significant. This means that those carrying out the traditions may not be consciously aware of the change. Therefore, even if a tradition undergoes major changes over many generations, it will be seen as unchanged.

Regarding loss, the terms *tradition* and *custom* are seen as synonymous. Both are established by long practice and especially by accepted conventions. A tradition is seen as the accepted standard that regulates individual behavior for a member of a social group. It defines a distinctive, expected practice. Traditions pass down elements of a culture or group from generation to generation, and mark a mode of thought or behavior that is continually followed by a group of people. Traditions and customs generally appear in the presence of life's punctuation marks, such as graduations, weddings, or birthdays, and are used to ground the group in the presence of change. This is also true of circumstances found in the customs of death and last rites.

One woman who had moved to a new region of the country told this story. "We moved here several years ago for my husband's new job and thought that we fit fairly well into the urban area. He got diagnosed with stomach cancer and had a pretty tough time with it. After 18 months, he died. We had some good, new friends who were able to help with things during chemotherapy and then at his end-of-life. But when my husband died, people started telling me about how things were 'done' in this community. Where I grew up, which is a long way away, it was the family's job to feed people after the funeral. Here, it was the other way around – people brought food to us. Then there were other folks who asked me if I needed help with flowers. I didn't plan to place a blanket of flowers on the casket, and that seemed to be very odd to the locals who attended the funeral. Some people wanted to know about the wake, which I hadn't planned either. Everybody had their own practices of what they considered the 'right way' to have a funeral. I felt like I was swimming upstream most of the time anyway, and had a really hard time trying to honor my family's traditions, rather than everyone else's."

Rituals are fundamentally different from habits and traditions. A ritual is a discrete set of actions, preformed for symbolic value, which may or may not be prescribed by the traditions of a community. Rituals address the human urge to comprehend existence in a meaningful way. The term refers to actions that are stylized and have highly personal value to those involved. A ritual is performed on a specific occasion, underscores the passage between two stages and articulates the search for a marked pathway as a person moves from one life stage to another. The voice of the ritual speaks to the human need to establish secure and fulfilling relationships within a human community, and holds the longing to acknowledge the past with great mystery.

The purposes of rituals are varied, though there are common themes that are woven through such discrete events. A ritual defines membership of the participants involved in the event, supporting the spiritual and emotional needs of its practitioners. A meaningful ritual strengthens the social bonds among members and defines the nature of affiliation between participants. These bonds nourish interpersonal relationships and confirm a participant's inclusion in the community. Healing is present in ritual activity. A numinous, respectful spirit musters during the unfolding of the ritual, oftentimes associated with atonement, purification, and dedication. Rituals are designed for expression of belief, and are often used in the context of worship. A ritual has a close connection to the sense of reverence; it is closely aligned with an idealized state of humanity, often expressed in a religious context. Finally, rituals are designed for the celebration and pleasure of the event itself. For the participant, the ritual is a spirited acknowledgement of a unique, meaningful place for finding one's self.

Good rituals are created and hold the five essential themes previously discussed, including membership, healing, identity, belief expression, and celebration. A ritual has meaning when it corresponds to the life transition it seeks to underline. While a ritual may borrow elements from ceremonies, traditions, and customs, it has its own definition and must be constructed in a highly personal, idiosyncratic way. There are six elements defining a potent ritual.

The first element is philosophical: A good ritual expresses the unexpressed. Most of ritual work is symbolic. Symbols express inner experiences, feelings, thoughts, or beliefs as if they were sensory experiences or events in the outer world. Symbols have different logic from conscious thought. Day-to-day conscious living is largely defined by time and space. In symbolic process, intensity and association are more relevant. Symbols express idea rather than fact, and a ritual is sensitive to what is unknown or difficult to define using concrete language. While a symbol does indeed have a concrete aspect, which is conscious and expressed through common language or object, the metaphor of a symbol serves as a bridge to what is alive in the unconscious. This suggests that symbols, by definition, are vague and ambiguous, fully open to interpretation. They cannot be precisely interpreted by any one single meaning. Symbols in rituals are given life and energy so that their meaning can continue. They are to be defined and used as signs for what cannot otherwise be expressed.

The second element of a good ritual is found in its service as a reference point for transitions. The metaphor of a psychological punctuation mark has been described in earlier discussion. Rituals mark differences and describe the shift from "that was then" to "this is now and this is what it means." An organized, enacted activity marks 'place', allowing full psychological and spiritual meaning to be observed, defined, and held. A ritual is about personal change. Therefore, what may be a tradition to some may be elevated to ritual status for others. A funeral serves as an example. For a funeral director, a service honors community and religious traditions associated with burying the dead. While the service and associated activities hold the custom and tradition, they are not always personal for the professional tasks that a staff must provide to those who collectively mourn. However, when a funeral director attends to the death of a loved one, such as a parent or spouse, the funeral takes on more of a symbolic, personal nature. It becomes a ritual and will be remembered as something special and unique to the survivor's memory of the deceased.

The third element of a good ritual is found in its capacity to build connective tissue to the self and between others. While ritual activities may certainly be created and enacted in private, a witness to the process generally serves to intensify the experience. A good ritual provides a framework for an individual to re-evaluate beliefs, priorities, and circumstances. Particularly with loss, there is a sense of exposure that leaves an individual feeling some degree of psychological nakedness. Re-examination of experience allows for a sense of recovering in an honest, congruent way that is grounding.

Fourth, a good ritual legitimizes new social relationships and life circumstances. A story will illustrate. A couple had been married for nearly thirty years, and the husband died suddenly in an automobile accident. The man's widow told her adult children, "I'll never marry again." She grieved mightily; after several years, she began to recognize the integration of the loss. Her husband's best friend, also a widower, had been a primary source of comfort as the woman dealt over the years with the demands exacted by the loss. Over time, they began to have romantic feelings toward each other, though the woman reported feeling guilty and "still married." Her guilt lead her to a course of grief therapy with a psychologist. In her therapy work, she was able to reconcile and integrate the loss in her memories of a good marriage and a family that had moved well through its developmental challenges and crises. She decided that she would like to pursue a more romantic relationship with her friend, but had difficulty, as she said, "putting things in place. There were too many strings hanging." The friend was a good man, able to hear and respect her difficulties, though he clearly stated his desires to take their relationship into a new level of intimacy.

With the assistance of her therapist, a ritual was created. The woman talked with her adult children and spouses and received their blessings for her wish. She was able to locate the minister who married her and her now deceased husband. With the minister's help, a ceremony was constructed. On a bright, spring day, the widow, her friend, and her family gathered in the living room. She stood before the minister and repeated her wedding vows taken decades before. When she spoke the promise of "till death do us part," she removed her wedding ring. The minister said a lovely prayer of peace and remembrance and offered hope for a bright future. No longer identified primarily as a widow, the woman and her friend entered into a new stage of their relationship that felt legitimate and congruent with her stage of life.

The fifth attribute of a meaningful ritual is defined by its ability to take us out of the everyday. A good ritual is unique to time, place, and circumstance. This characteristic marks it as different from a tradition, which can be repeated and serves as a woven thread through culture and family, repeated over time. The ritual is numinous, and as such, should have mystery, symbol, and ceremony. Understanding and comprehending the good ritual happens at a sensual, bone level.

The final component defining a good ritual is its ability to strengthen the meaning in change. The wedding ceremony described earlier provides a lovely illustration of this. The widow was moving in an unencumbered way through the territory of grief and found new, unexpected parts of herself that had reawakened. Even with conscious and mindful acknowledgement of the change, she was unable to fully claim her capacity for a new, intimate relationship. The organization and orchestration of the ritual provided a grounding event to strengthen her resolve and sense of self.

Rituals are constructed for an appropriate point of transition. The participants in the ritual should be invited to collaborate in its preparation and enactment. Its design is best approached in a simple, meaningful way. The more elaborate the ritual, the more likely the meaning will be blurred or lost in the ceremony. Enactment of the ritual, allowing participation from all who serve as witness, enhances its meaning-making capacity. The ritual is approached and performed in a sacred way, and is designated as the "punctuation" point for the transition. A grief counselor described the ritual process, saying, "A good ritual connects the mind, body, and spirit. The mind conceives it, the body performs it, and the spirit stands witness to it."

FUNERALS

The word funeral comes from the Latin *fumus*, which has multiple meanings, including references to the corpse and the last rites themselves. A funeral is a ceremony for celebrating, respecting, or sanctifying the life of a person who has died. The funeral provides mourners a context of meaning as death is integrated into personal religious and philosophical frameworks. Funeral customs constitute the constellation of beliefs and practices used by a culture or society to remember the dead, from the interment itself to various prayers, services, and monuments undertaken in their honor. A funeral is designed to bind the social group together through present experience and collective memory, and affirm the social order "by offering testimony that despite the death that has occurred, the community lives on" (Rando, 1984).

Customs of last rites vary widely among cultures and religious affiliations within cultures, though all traditions express a communal belief in the conveyance of value and belief regarding the meaning of life and death. There are cultures and world religions in which the funeral is seen as a vehicle for preparing the dead to successfully migrate into the afterlife or afterworld. Traditional western customs are focused on the welfare of the survivors. Socially, a funeral provides a setting for the bereaved system to make a public statement that one of its members has died. The wider community then uses the occasion to respond with sympathy and support. Historically, the funeral has addressed four major social functions:

1. It serves to acknowledge and commemorate a person's death.

2. It provides a setting for the disposition of the dead body.

3. It assists in reorienting the bereaved to their lives, which have been ruptured by the death.

4. It demonstrates reciprocal economic and social obligations between the bereaved and their social world. (Pine, 1995)

Funeral traditions serve to bolster the solidarity of the social group and family system. The system is connected to the society as a whole and is regulated by the organization of the culture and the membership of the group. In many ways, the system reifies the psychosocial tasks exacted by loss. Quickly, following a death, a social necessity musters to address the needs of the survivors and surrounding social group. This seems to be a social mandate. "Since mortality tends to disrupt the ongoing life and social groups and relationships, all societies must develop some forms of containing its impact" (Blauner, 1966, p. 378). The funeral proceedings provide meaningful, structured sets of activities that counter the secondary loss of predictability and order that frequently accompany the death of a loved one. The rites prescribe a defined social role and suggest tasks for a time when self-directed actions and purposeful behavior become elusive. An apt description of the social functions of funeral rites comes from Herman Feifel's edited work, *The Meaning of Death*:

Certain things must be done after a death, whether it occurs in a very simple or in a highly complex society. The corpse must be disposed of; those who are bereaved – who are personally shocked and socially disoriented – must be helped to reorient themselves;

the whole group must have a known way of readjustment after
the loss of one of its members. These things "must" be done in the
sense that they *are* done. When people find that they have no set
pattern for dealing with death – as may occur in newly coalesced
groups – or when they discover that the former pattern is no longer
a feasible one, they tend quickly to establish some clear plan for
coping with the occasion of death. (Mandelbaum, 1959, p. 189)

The way in which cultures develop funeral customs and traditions is
described by Pine (1969):

Death gives rise to immediate personal emotional responses which
seem to trigger certain culturally oriented responses and reactions
which evolve into specific patterns of bereavement. Every culture
has deeply entrenched traditional customs for handling death, and
as grief ensues, societally-based reactions become more pronounced
in the form of funeral practices. These customary practices aim at
providing meaningful structures upon which bereaved people may
lean, hopefully giving them some sense of consolation and easing
the transition caused by the termination of personal interaction.
(p. 62)

Psychologically, the funeral provides scaffolding for survivors who are
coming to concrete and literal terms with the loss and physical absence of
the deceased. The funeral confirms and reinforces the reality of death. In
moving through funeral rites, there is active acknowledgement and expression
of feelings of loss, aiding survivors in focusing the energy associated with the
developmental and psychological tasks and processes that engage those coping
strategies personally addressing the loss. Funerals assist mourners in early
stages of accommodation to the changed relationship between themselves
and the deceased loved one. The funeral stimulates the recollection of the
deceased and begins the process of moving the deceased from the physical
to memory.

Whatever funeral rites are adopted, they must be personally meaningful
to the bereaved. Those that have no meaning to the bereaved have little healing
value, where those that are meaningful are perceived as positive components
of the grieving process. There is long-standing research that supports the
critical psychological and sociological importance with funeral rites and full
participation in them (Volkan, 1975). Later research supports the value of

the funeral and associated last rites, as reported by Therese Rando (1984), who said:

> Subjects who participated in what would be termed a "traditional" funeral (i.e., who viewed the body and who involved their friends and relatives in the ceremony) reported fewer adjustment problems, more positive recall of the deceased, and closer ties and warmer relationships with their relatives than did subjects who had less than the traditional funeral. The funeral seemed to bring the surviving members closer together. A greater sense of urgency with respect to being kind and considerate of other survivors was reported. Those who did not view the body or had arranged for immediate disposition of the remains (excluding the normal Jewish custom of not viewing the body) reported the greatest hostility following the death; the greatest increase in consumption of alcohol, tranquilizers, and sedatives; the greatest increase in tension and anxiety; the lowest positive recall of the deceased; and greater problems in adjustment to the death, particularly among male respondents. (p. 191)

Last rites and other mourning traditions and rituals have the great potential to facilitate resolution of grief. However, if the purposes of the rites are distorted, resolution of grief is more difficult. Therefore, it is useful to separate errors of interpretation from the usefulness and utility of the design. Such rites hold proven value in providing a good beginning for the uncomplicated grieving process. As Thomas Lynch, author of *The Undertaking: Life Studies from the Dismal Trade* (1997) said, "Funerals are the way we close the gap between the death that happens and the death that matters" (p. 21).

MULTICULTURAL CONSIDERATIONS IN LIFE AND LOSS

All people who experience the death of a loved or close one feel a personal and social sense of upset and distress. This imbalance lasts for extended periods of time. However, when it comes to the specifics of characterizing that state of being out of sorts and disabled, there are many diverse emotional expressions found across cultures. It is also common that what is grieved after a death is not just the one specific loss of a person, but more secondary losses that will present over time. These losses tally up, including unfinished business with the deceased, loss of role functioning and role relationship, and loss of innocence about mortality. Across cultures, death rips a hole in the social fabric of the system. These holes are difficult to repair, and from culture to culture, the ruptures of the social fabric and their significance vary widely.

Culture is defined as a social construction. It includes a shared and distinctive identity, as well as a set of practices, language, and beliefs that demarcate it from other surrounding cultures. Cultural ideas give a sense of propriety to grief and bereavement practices, and are in constant operation during last rites. This is true even in situations where there are less obvious and overt cultural dictates regarding formal expressions of mourning. Social ceremonies of death vary in elaboration, time and enactment, and economic costs of performance. All such events offer the bereaved cultural meanings that help define and integrate the meaning of the loss. That being said, a culture is not a unitary entity. In most cultures, there is a great deal of diversity existing in beliefs, customs, rituals, practices, language usage, and engagement with the culture. The diversity is revealed through idiosyncratic family practices, in disagreements people and groups within the culture have about appropriate behavior and tradition, and in attempts to understand or explain varied aspects of life and death.

Most people carry multiple cultures in their psychological understanding of the self. A family of origin may include more than one culture. As individual members mature, are educated, have religious conversions, move to a new geographic location, or learn a new language, there is a broadening of cultural diversity within the system. Such challenges unfold in the bereavement process by coming to terms with differing norms, meanings, ways of expressing feelings, and ideals for tradition and ritual activities. Because cultural processes are fluid and not static, the changing variations invite participants to learn and unlearn different understandings and social proprieties in the midst of the adverse circumstances related to the death of a loved one.

Across cultures, groups give meaning to death, arising in substantial part from the ethnicity, language, and social relationships of those members of the group. It is not a simple matter to come to meaning about a death, which is multi-layered and extends across individual, family, and community definitions. Considerable variations unfold in how the grieving process is experienced and expressed. Embracing a multicultural perspective offers the bereaved individual a sense of common humanity with all grieving people and a sense that the particular culture contains highly stylized and a personally relevant means of expression.

The author Paul Rosenblatt (2003) suggests that the study of life and loss across cultures raises six key questions that should be considered in order to be culturally sensitive in entering the system of the bereaved. They include:

1. What is life and what is death?
2. What is grieved as death?
3. Why did the death occur?
4. What is lost because of the death?
5. What is normal grieving?
6. What does the culture allow and provide for a person who is grieving?

In order to appreciate personal and others' responses to loss and death, an understanding of the social and cultural context within which they occur is crucial. Because death is universal, each culture has developed its own beliefs, mores, norms, standards, and restrictions. Each society dictates the standards to be followed, supporting or prohibiting certain behaviors and determining the repertoire of responses from which mourners may choose. Any contact with those in the area of life and loss must take into account the social, cultural, religious/philosophical, and ethnic backgrounds. Consideration of these variables provides a more complete understanding of the social and cultural framework out of which the bereaved system will operate. An appreciation of this will strongly influence the clarity with which the system can express itself.

VIII

Life, Loss, Ethics, and the Law

Death is beautiful when seen to be a law, and not an accident–It is as common as life.

Henry David Thoreau

Mors sceptraligonibusaequat. (Death levels sceptre and the law.)
Unattributed Author, inscribed over a 14th century
mural painting once at Battle Church, Sussex

The difference between right and wrong? Wrong is worse, right?
Sipress cartoon, circa 2005

This chapter is a bit of a diversion, since it speaks to issues related to those who will continue to live. Rather than speaking about bereavement, this speaks to those who seriously consider mortality as an issue of life and one that should be addressed with eyes wide open. As such, any full discussion of life and loss must consider the notions of ethics and the law. Ethics is the branch of philosophy that involves systematizing, defending, and recommending concepts of right and wrong conduct. In philosophy, ethics studies moral behavior in humans and how one should act. The word ethic comes from the Greek *ethos*, meaning character. As a discipline, ethics is divided into four major areas of study:

- Meta-ethics: The theoretical meaning and reference of moral propositions and how their truth values (if any) may be determined
- Normative ethics: The practical means of determining a moral course of action

96

- Applied ethics: How moral outcomes can be achieved in specific situations

- Descriptive ethics, also known as comparative ethics: The study of people's beliefs about morality

Law is defined by the authoritative principles and regulations established in a community. The law is generally applicable to its people as a whole, whether in the form of legislation or of customs and policies recognized and enforced by judicial decision. To effectively address life and loss from the perspective of ethics and the law, attention must be placed on multiple issues, all revolving around maturity and judgment. As T.S. Eliot wrote, "… the mind of God in me shows what it is time to move on to and what it is time to let go of. What we call the beginning is often the end and to make an end is to make a beginning; the end is where we start from" (1936, p. 38). With the paradigm shift regarding approaches to grief and bereavement, new considerations must be examined to meet the needs of those individuals, both patient and caregiver, struggling with issues surrounding death and dying.

Advances in managing and treating acute, life-threatening illnesses have led to greater longevity and give rise to ethical and humane concerns about the prospect of longer, medicalized, and impersonal deaths. In the current western zeitgeist, there is progressively more interest in a greater degree of self-determination rather than the old-fashioned notion of "we're doing this for your own good." Choice and autonomy are considered paramount in all decisions related to life and loss. In recent times, public concern about the legal aspects of death and dying have been more figural, and have become focused in three primary areas: Defining death in a way that responds to the realities of contemporary life-sustaining technology at end-of-life, communicating wishes concerning medical interventions at end-of-life, and sanctioning healthcare assistance in terminating life when further care is futile.

Any discussion of ethics and the law must carefully consider end-of-life care decisions. Despite the devolving healthcare system in the United States, advances in medicine and public health have extended life expectancy, though the quality of life remains an issue. The average life expectancy worldwide has risen from 48 years in 1955 to 65 years in 1995 to 70 years in 2008. In the United States, the average life expectancy has increased from 47 years in 1900 to a record high of 78.0 in 2011 (National Center for Health Statistics, 2011). Quality of life has emerged as being as important an issue as longevity. More directly regarding life and loss, the initial ethical issue initially revolves around the definition of death. A detailed discussion of the criteria related to the definition of death is found in Chapter 2.

What is relevant in the ethics discussion is that symbolically, the "moment of death" is no longer momentous. Deathbed scenes throughout history have held religious implications related to sin, purification of the soul and redemption, all of which occurred close to the moment of dying. Biological human life "…has value as a means, a precondition for specifically human activities of a human person. This value makes us face the crucial question of what activities are specifically human, such that lacking these or a reasonable hope of regaining them back makes biological human life cease to have value to anyone" (Garrett, Baillie, & Garrett, 2010, p. 188). Because of medical advances, there are multiple decision points regarding treatment options to maintain or extend life. It is now possible to artificially postpone the moment of death by sustaining, supplanting, or restoring vital functions. Fortunately, bigger questions arise: What are the minimal factors that give life a value to the patient? What is the threshold of meaningfulness of human life to its possessor?

Until the middle 1980s, these questions were left to the physician and healthcare team to answer. Now, the decisions are morally and ethically made by the patient and his or her intimate system. All medical and social service codes of conduct say that these types of decisions are highly subjective and depend on clinical evidence about the quality of life. In the medical and social service vernacular, the terms 'clinical' and 'observable' are synonymous. Therefore, as stated by Therese Rando (1984,) healthcare professionals should:

> …be aware of the personal and subjective values that may contribute to evaluations of quality of life…Clinical decisions that hinge on assessing quality of life should be undertaken with great care and full cognizance of the subjectivity of the assessment, with full patient participation, or, if that is not possible, with participation of knowledgeable and concerned relatives or guardians. (p. 183)

Later, in 2005, emphasis was added in the *Ethics Manual of the American College of Physicians* with the statement saying, "Family members and health care workers should avoid projecting their own values or view about quality of life onto the incapacitated patient. Quality of life should be assessed according to the patient's perspective" (2005, p. 189). These types of discussions of quality of life fall under the domain of applied ethics.

Applied ethics is the philosophical examination, from a moral standpoint, of issues in private life, such as quality of life, that are matters of moral judgment. It is different from the field of *normative ethics*, which is concerned with what people should believe to be right or wrong, and extends to more pragmatic and personal evaluations. *Applied ethics* focuses on situation and circumstance, rather than being directed entirely by theory. This branch of ethics deals with hard choices – the kind found in the presence of issues of life and loss.

Psychologists James and Elizabeth Bugental assert that in our humanity there are two fundamental "givens." They write: "Humans have the capacity of acting or not acting, and humans have choice" (1984, p. 543). It is out of choice that people create meaning. Choice and control are vital to personal sanity, even in the presence of death. Therefore, the greater the sense of autonomy and decision- making allowed and facilitated in life and loss considerations, the greater the quality of life that is afforded.

As noted by the Supreme Court in discussions begun in the late 19th century: "No right is held more sacred, or is more carefully guarded by the common law, than the right of every individual to the possession and control of his own person. Free from all restraint or interference from others, unless by clear and unquestionable authority of law" (Union Pacific Co. v. Botsford, 1981). Autonomy, synonymous with self-governance, is defined as, "…one ought to respect a competent person's choices, where one can do so without undue cost to oneself, where to do so will not violate other moral obligations, and where these choices do not threaten harm to other persons or parties" (Battin, 1994, p. 5). Inherent in the definition is the notion that competent individuals have the right to accept or refuse treatment. This definition holds a strong component of self-determination, but may force individuals into choices they would rather not make. Therefore, the obligation of healthcare is to respect the autonomous choice of individuals and to foster it appropriately as a right without insisting on it as a duty.

It cannot be overstated that the right to choose is a paramount moral value, and those involved with patients, caregivers, or bereaved members of the system are obligated to help weigh options rather than prescribe a course of action. The degree of choice varies depending on the individual's independence and cognitive capacity. The notion of choice is particularly relevant for survivors who complete advance directives. Advance directives promote shared decision-making, as they secure the individual's right to informed consent or informed refusal of treatment. Choice is based on diagnosis, prognosis, treatment options, risks and benefits of treatment, and what is curative and what is life-sustaining.

Most Americans, when asked, say they would not want to be kept alive artificially by medical interventions if they suffered from a terminal illness or had severe dementia. A 2003 study by the Agency for Healthcare Research and Quality (ARHQ) found that nearly 72% of respondents would refuse cardiopulmonary resuscitation, mechanical respiration, intravenous fluids, and artificial nutrition if they had dementia. Those numbers rose to higher than 82% when respondents were asked to assume they had dementia and a terminal illness (ARHQ, 2003). However, fewer than 50% of individuals in the United States have expressed their wishes through advance directives. In the ARHQ study, only 12% of people who have executed advance directives have discussed them with their healthcare professionals, and over 65% of physicians are unaware if their patients have actually executed their advance directives (ARHQ, 2003).

ADVANCE DIRECTIVES

Advance directives give an individual clear choices and control. They are instructions that direct health care providers regarding personal and reasoned wishes related to life support, efforts to revive a stopped heart or breathing, nutrition and hydration, and pain management. Without such directives, a medical care giving team may be legally bound to do everything available to sustain life until a responsible surrogate decides otherwise. Such directives are best written before an emergency presents itself. Advance care planning helps prepare for death and opens discussion with relevant members of an individual's support system and network. Advance directives ensure that death will take place in a manner consistent with individual values and wishes. The conversation surrounding advance directives enhances a system's sense of control and well-being during critical times. Decisions should be placed in writing using advance directive forms and shared with others. Some of the most ethically challenging situations are faced by families, healthcare, and social service professionals when no discussion regarding treatment preferences at the end of life have occurred between patients and families or between patients and their healthcare providers.

Advance directives are intended to extend the individual's autonomy to a time when she becomes incapacitated or incompetent due to a debilitating illness or condition. All fifty states have passed statutes protecting the use of advance directives, although the form of the instructions and exact sanctions regarding their use varies from state to state. The first state to enact an advance directive law, the Natural Death Law, was California in 1976. The statute was stimulated by the situation faced by the well-known case of Karen Ann Quinlan. Ms. Quinlan's father pursued judicial means to authorize the removal of life supports from his daughter. The case was landmark, since the 1976 iteration of the state law would not have applied to the Quinlan case. The California law only covered incapacitated individuals whose death was imminent, not those expecting a prolonged dying process, which is the fear of many people. Ultimately, a federal policy known as the Patient Self-Determination Act became effective at the end of 1991. The act was aimed at promoting the use of advance directives, with the new law giving recognition to the pluralistic and democratic ideals of the United States and the belief that the individual has the right to choose how to live, therefore the right to choose how to die.

In general, advance directives have seven necessary characteristics for useful instructions:

1. Instructions should correspond as closely as possible to questions most likely to arise in the care of seriously ill, mentally incompetent persons.

2. Instructions should be clear.

3. Future states should be anticipated.

4. Whether individuals would want the advance directive followed if there is a change or a partial or full recovery versus if recovery seems remote.

5. Whether withdrawal of various types of life support is indicated, if individuals were to encounter a situation where they would want treatment stopped.

6. Whether withdrawal of invasive life-sustaining treatments, such as nutrition and hydration, is desired.

7. Advance directives should only be completed by individuals who thoroughly understand the content and the implications of their instructions (Culver, 1998).

A *living will* is an advance directive to the physician regarding the dying individual's feelings about the use of life-support equipment or other extraordinary measures to sustain life. It is recognized as a legal document in all states. However, the use of living wills has constraints. The individual must ask and answer the question "If I become terminally ill and permanently incompetent, do I want all medical treatment withheld or withdrawn?" Given the wide range of interventions now available, a living will leaves a fair amount of ambiguity that does not provide the specificity that will guide effective decision- making without additional direction. The living will speaks to the definition of "terminally and incurably ill." Benchmarks for meeting the definition focus on the patient's suffering from an illness for which no known measures are effective in reversing its course, or whose course has progressed beyond the capacity of existing knowledge or techniques to arrest it. In this context, death would occur within days or weeks unless extraordinary means were employed.

Given the limits to a living will, it is advisable for an individual to appoint a caregiver or intimate as a healthcare proxy who is legally designated to make decisions about treatment and medical care. The document addressing this is called a *healthcare power-of-attorney.* It is a legal document, where named individuals are expected to ensure that individuals' directives are carried out. Because not all situations can be specified in advance, the surrogates are trusted to use substituted judgment, defined legally by the "best interest standard" to make appropriate decisions regarding medical treatment. The individual's representative attempts to determine whether the patient would have consented to or refused treatment, and is marked by three reference points: the expressed wishes of the individual, the known value system, and any other reliable evidence of the patient's wishes.

A third type of directive is a *Do Not Resuscitate (DNR)* order, also known as a "no code." The DNR conveys a physician's order that a dying individual should not receive cardiopulmonary resuscitation if the patient stops breathing and/or the heart stops beating.

These three advance directives giving specific instructions to the attending physician, healthcare team, and caregivers should be easily accessible. The documents maintain the dying individual's choice, control, and dignity, and allay the healthcare team's fear of liability by minimizing litigious risk. Conversations about death and dying can be held using advance directives as a stimulus. These are difficult discussions to have for most people, since they involve highly personal values and choices, such as desire for artificial feeding, use of pain medications, and whether or not resuscitation and ventilation are desired. Many, if not most, people will avoid such conversations. However, as one family member said, following her mother's death, "Most advance directives don't say anything specific enough about care. For our family, the papers were in the wrong place at the wrong time. My siblings and I had different ideas about what our mother wanted, and they conflicted with our very different value systems. We never had the talk we should've had as a group. If we had been able to sit down and talk it through when our mother was healthier, it would have been more like a trial run. As it was, by the time I located all of the right papers, several decisions had been made that went against her wishes, and her death was much more difficult for her and contentious for us than was necessary. After my mother died, my husband and I did our advance directives, sat down with our young adult children, and made it clear as a bell about our wishes…and where our papers would be filed." This woman's concerns are valid. Family members and healthcare providers often guess wrong about what their loved ones or patients would want if faced with terminal illnesses or severe dementia. The aforementioned study found that physicians were accurate in predicting patient preferences only about 65% of the time and tended to provide less treatment than their patients would otherwise have requested. Surrogates who were family members, on the other hand, tended to authorize more treatment than the patient would have otherwise preferred, even if the patient and the surrogate had previously reviewed or discussed the patient's advance directives (ARHQ, 2003).

The final advance directive is the *last will and testament*, a legal document stating an individual's wishes for the settlement of his or her estate after death. A will is the best way to determine the distribution of personal belongings and assets, to provide for family needs regarding underage children, to plan wisely for taxes, and to make charitable contributions. Only by having a will can the individual be assured that personal wishes will be carried out after death.

MEDICAL FUTILITY

The goal of medicine is to heal, restore, "to make whole," or provide a benefit to patients. Healthcare's obligation is to forestall untimely death and to relieve suffering. Whenever possible, its goal is to treat to cure and bring about a full functional recovery. It does not include offering treatments that do not produce benefits (Schneiderman, Jecker, & Jonsen, 1996). At end of life, there comes a time when disease will overcome medicine. The ethical shift of attention at this point moves care toward palliation of discomfort and assistance in coping with the demands of illness, progressive disability, and dying. To treat to cure is abandoned as a goal of intervention.

Medical futility is defined as "any effort to provide a benefit to a patient that is highly likely to fail and which, except in rare instances, cannot be systematically produced" (Schneiderman, et al., 1996, p. 8). It is recognized as the use of interventions that will fail to restore patients to health and function. Futility is defined by the effectiveness, benefits, and burdens of treatment.

Effectiveness refers to the ability of the treatment to produce a change in the course of the disease. This is a judgment made by the clinician/physician. A clinical judgment that a medical intervention is futile provides a sound basis for declining the recommendation of an extraordinary or heroic intervention. However, by contemporary ethic, perceived benefits of treatment are ultimately to be determined solely by patients and refer to the patient's conception of what the results could mean to them.

The notion of "burden" holds objective and subjective factors, and involves consideration of the cost, pain, discomfort, and inconvenience of the procedure and the individual's assessment of quality of life. Burden is defined as an action intended to benefit others, and is fundamental to the purpose and rationale of healthcare. It is balanced with autonomy in terms of priority. Burden implies an interpersonal transaction, requiring conversation and consideration between the patient, caregiver, and healthcare team. It is derived from the fiduciary relationship between the patient and treatment provider, with the fundamental understanding that the purpose of treatment is to meet the health needs and promote the well-being of the individual, however subjectively defined. Without clear understandings of what each considers burdensome, assumptions are made that, at the very best, will be inaccurate, and at the worst, will be altogether wrong. Again, these decisions at end of life ethically lie in the autonomy of the individual. "Physicians may not unilaterally decide the quality of another person's life, use age as a sole criterion, or invoke economics without reference to the question of futility" (Pelligrino, 2000, p. 1067). Ethically, the greater principle of mercy is also applied to the notion of futility. The principle speaks to the duty to relieve or end suffering that is currently occurring. While it should not contravene the individual's wishes, it is invoked as a justification for end-of-life decisions that could result in hastening death.

Futility comes from the Latin word meaning "leaky." Futile treatments serve no meaningful purpose, no matter how often they are repeated. The likelihood of success is very small and the patient's quality of life is unacceptable. All involved in decision-making believe that the prospective benefit is not worth the resources required to intervene. The word is well chosen. Even with the availability of educational materials related to end of life care, advance directives, and medical futility, the message is clear: Many years after the passage of the federal mandate of the Patient Self-Determination Act of 1990, which was designed to ensure that individuals are informed about their end of life decision making rights, most Americans still do not adequately plan for and communicate their preferences regarding end of life care.

Death casts a long shadow in contemporary society, one which most typically refuse to notice. As death approaches, many people are stunned and feel unprepared to deal with the situation and circumstances of death, dying, grief, and loss. However, the graying of society and the politicization of end of life care make the issues increasingly relevant. Basic knowledge of advance directives, heroic measures, and the ethics of informed consent help with the realization of the tasks and decisions associated with a meaningful ending to life and death with dignity.

IX

Special Issues

Loss wasn't – mustn't be, couldn't be – an end in itself. It had to mean something. But finding out its meaning was like scaling a gigantic wall. Was it there just so I could get over it?

Susanna Tamaro, *Follow Your Heart*

Sometimes death leaps suddenly upon its victims like a thug.

Robert Louis Stevenson, *Aes Triplex*

For most people, death seems relatively distant. However, there is salience in exploring some of the more figural issues related to life and loss when an unexpected death is thrust into the face of an individual, family, or community. While there are age-related and individual differences that exist in the awareness and response to death, meanings are also rooted in historical events which shape individual and cultural responses.

As humans, there is a need to find a satisfactory explanation for the loss of a loved one. This cognitive and philosophical acceptance is one of the fundamental processes involved in grief integration and recovery. Integration occurs in an individual's frame of reference. People's understanding of important life events and their implications are social constructs and operate in response to collective values, morals, and folkways. Individuals find meaning in idiosyncratic, highly personal ways. Families typically demonstrate this sense of collective meaning-making in storytelling about the loss; the system searches for commonalities in personal understandings of the events or meanings surrounding the death. Communities will explore the meaning of death on a larger scale. These efforts focus on the healing of the community as well as reaffirming its purpose and a renewal of a favorable and optimistic sense of the future.

While this chapter is by no means inclusive in the special issues related to life and loss, discussions about certain types of losses that involve social and communal processes may provide general roadmaps and guides for meaning-making, understanding, and integrating the many variables that influence a conscious and mindful appreciation of life and loss.

EUTHANASIA AND ASSISTED DEATH

Also known as rational suicide, this has been an ethics issue for years, and certainly impacts the discussions surrounding life and loss. Death, when considered from the context of a patient's end-of-life or the bereaved's perspective as survivor, turns an individual toward a personally felt sense of humanity and vulnerability. As has been stated, death can be deferred by life-sustaining technology. While the law of the land supports heroic and extraordinary care, it does not allow for interventions that would actively cause death. Acknowledging this fact, all competent individuals have a right to refuse any medical treatment, even if such a refusal might result in death. The confounding question of medical futility arises when the healthcare team may disagree with the patient or surrogate's decision about how to proceed. This circumstance holds the potential to bring about a psychological face-off between the expertise of the healthcare provider and the autonomy of the patient. The question arises: Can the patient or surrogate choose or demand treatment that goes contrary to expert advice for healing or palliation? The question underlines the fundamental notion of autonomy. Such choice focuses attention on the ultimate dichotomous choice: to continue with futile treatment or make an active choice to end life. Both ends of the continuum, framed by the choices, are complicated.

Considerations regarding the voluntary ending of life are among the most profound secrets kept when considering loss. Family members, friends, social service, and medical professionals may find themselves in discussions of this deeply personal issue, including the process regarding deciding to end life, the search for an acceptable means, and the actual incidence of death. These kinds of conversations bring new, uncomfortable, and complex problems for all concerned. Euthanasia comes from the origin of the word meaning "good death." It is seen as an active process, though paradoxically can be passively facilitated when an individual chooses to defer interventions that will sustain life. The conversations about euthanasia revolve around quality of life factors, which become more figural as a terminally ill individual considers a voluntary end of life. When a patient asks the healthcare team for a means that will bring about death, or even for the administration of such a means, the prevailing ethic and law are clear: Even if the individual is competent, the provider cannot assist in suicide. The law forbids help in assisted suicide, and the ethical nature of medicine is devoted to the obligation to heal. Even in the presence of these presumptions and obligations against cooperating in an assisted suicide, there are more cases than would be imagined in which neither healing nor comforting is possible. It is embedded in the psyche of western thought that autonomy is a key to the quality of life. Even with legal and ethical sanctions, such conversations frequently bubble to the surface and demand empathic and thoughtful engagement, all revolving around the notions contained in the definition of quality of life.

The first quality of life factor centers on the symptoms of an illness and how side effects of treatment become relevant. An example illustrates: A lay minister in a small southern town endured years of treatment for a variety of cancers that metastasized over the course of time. The fellow allowed draconian interventions to be made, relying strongly on his family and faith system for support. Eventually, the cancer involved his vocal cords. He gathered his family and said, "That's all. It is just enough. If I can't preach and teach, then my life's work is done. I'm refusing any more treatment." His family objected and asked the healthcare team to persuasively present options that would have extended the man's life, even though his speech production would be severely compromised regardless of the course of care. He steadfastly refused further treatments and died quickly as the cancer overtook his body.

The example ushers in the second quality of life factor and speaks to the individual's functional ability to perform basic activities of daily living. This can certainly be seen in the minister's life. The treatments offered for him would have taken away his ability to speak. Losing the functional capacity of speech was a greater price for longevity than the man was willing to bear. The dignity afforded by independence and ability to take care of oneself in basic ways is psychologically related to the sense of competence and esteem. As a person loses these capacities, the sense of "this is who I am" can quickly translate to "this is who I was," which can harshly affect mood and resilience.

The third quality of life factor speaks to individual experience of happiness, pleasure, pain, and suffering. These are all highly subjective states of being. The minister told his family, "I've had a good life, and I've been able to endure the cancer long enough to matter to you all and to others. I guess I could continue to see this thing through. But, you know, the pain has increased. I've not really suffered, though, because I've felt so many people's love and support. Now, enough is enough. I like to preach and teach, and to do that, I have to talk. If I can't, or it is too painful, then I'll be suffering. Love me enough now to let me go." Reluctantly, and with great sadness, the family complied with their loved one's wish to discontinue further treatment.

The final quality of life consideration factoring into the end-of-life equation hinges on the person's sense of independence, privacy, and dignity. After the minister's death, his physician revealed an interesting conversation to his adult daughter. "Your dad and I talked about assisted suicide. He really did not want to go through the pain of death if it could be prevented. We talked about pain medicines and how the body eventually shuts down, and he asked if there was anything that he could do to speed it up when the time was 'right.' He also asked me if I could speed it up for him if he couldn't make or tell me the decision." The doctor continued, saying, "I've had these kinds of conversations before. I would never help someone to end his life, but I can certainly listen to his wishes and talk about the process of how things will work out." In this case, the loss of dignity had to be accepted as a reality and dealt with in as real and potent a way as the physical disease. While the physician did not facilitate the minister's suicide, his availability to courageously listen and speak of the issue protected the man's rights and demonstrated compassionate care. The physician continued with the daughter, saying, "My professional obligation is always to heal. With your dad, my professional role butted up against the larger question of his human dignity. This took us into places that I still don't fully understand, and I have to let my conscience guide me as much as the ethics and the law. Our conversations gave us a chance to strengthen our bonds. Agreeing with your dad's decision to stop treatment was helpful to him at the end of his life. I have to believe that this was more healing to him than another round of chemotherapy."

Whether in agreement with euthanasia or facilitated suicide or not, the issues are emotionally, morally, and philosophically provocative. The idea that people should and can choose how they wish to live and therefore to die is fundamental to the integrity of autonomy and self-determination. The right to refuse treatment is widely recognized and accepted in health care today, including in end-of-life care decisions. For proponents of facilitated suicide, little difference exists between refusal of treatment, withdrawal of treatment, or deliberate overdose of medication. The continuum of care seems to be a logical extension for patients suffering and beyond cure.

The United States has engaged in a more public discussion regarding assisted death revolving around the question: If it is permissible to allow a patient to die without continuing care, why is it not permissible to help the patient to die? The uncertainties involved in the question beg for definitive answers. The most visible political solution has occurred in the state of Oregon. In 1994, passed by a slim margin, the Death with Dignity Act legalized physical-assisted suicide in the state. It was not implemented because of court appeals and was ultimately put back on a state ballot for possible repeal. In 1997, the repeal measure was rejected by 60 percent of the vote. The act remains controversial and is quite complicated. Under the law, a competent adult Oregon resident who has been diagnosed, by a physician, with a terminal illness that will lead to the death of the patient within six months, may request in writing, from his or her physician, a prescription for a lethal dose of medication for the purpose of ending the patient's life. Exercise of the option under this law is voluntary and the patient must initiate the request. Any physician, pharmacist, or healthcare provider who has moral objections may refuse to participate. The request must be confirmed by two witnesses, at least one of whom is not related to the patient and not entitled to any portion of the patient's estate, is not the patient's physician, and is not employed by a health care facility caring for the patient. After the request is made, another physician must independently examine the patient's medical records and confirm the diagnosis. The patient must be determined to be free of a mental condition impairing judgment. If the request is authorized, the patient must wait at least fifteen days and make a second oral request before the prescription may be written. The patient has a right to rescind the request at any time. Should either physician have concerns about the patient's ability to make an informed decision, or feel the patient's request may be motivated by depression or coercion, the patient must be referred for a psychological evaluation. The law protects doctors from liability for providing a lethal prescription for a terminally ill, competent adult in compliance with the statute's restrictions. Participation by physicians, pharmacists, and health care providers is voluntary. The law also specifies that a patient's decision to end life shall not "have an effect upon a life, health, or accident insurance or annuity policy."

Readers are reminded that this text is not meant to bring a full exposition, nor resolve the notion of the "slippery slope" related to the legalization of euthanasia and assisted death. It is meant to underline the truth that these discussions happen with more frequency than publically reported. Under any other circumstances, the literature discussing suicide considers self-destructive ideation as erupting from a temporary crisis, i.e., a perfect storm of time, place, and temperament, and that an individual who is irrationally considering death is unable to know and realize the prospects of continuing to live meaningfully on their own terms. There are many preferred interventions to help a suicidal individual move beyond the critical time where self-imposed death seems like a viable option. Terminal illness, though, is no temporary crisis. The suffering that it entails leaves an individual in the presence of the meaningful prospects of dying over living. While caregivers and healthcare professionals do not want to consider voluntary means of ending life, the terminally ill individual may exercise the right to contemplate and deliberate about suicidal actions. These thoughts and plans are not always irrational; therefore, the presumptions of need to remove an individual's rights of choice are less relevant than they would be in other circumstances. When an individual is known to be in command of his or her faculties, deciding and acting in ways that express the true self, without coercion, brings the notion of autonomy back into focus. Therefore, the issue is not one of when or whether it is not appropriate to take measures to keep another from carrying out a decision about suicide, but more when it is or is not appropriate to support another in considering and possibly carrying out such a decision.

COMMUNITY VIOLENCE AND DISASTER

In the last two decades, there has been increasing interest in the effects of traumatic events, including community violence and natural disasters, on people and societies. The world seems to be in a dynamic and constant state of mayhem. Natural and human-made tragedies, including actions of humans directed against other humans, have profound impact on grief, bereavement, life, and loss. When an individual death is expected, the anticipation of the event sets in motion a process for how intimates and friends in the system will grieve, since grief and mourning are basic human responses that unfold in relatively predictable, culturally defined ways. When a disaster strikes that produces great loss, there is a collective form of mourning. Violent and disastrous events affect social understandings of death and dying as well as grief, bereavement, and mourning processes. The reactions to death are felt at individual, community, and societal levels, and clearly affect others in ways that are beyond what would be typically be felt from the loss of a known loved one. These events present countless problems for communities as they seek to find adequate social responses to great loss of life resulting from the adverse effects of tragedy. Normative responses seem inadequate for dealing with such losses.

Certainly the most potent image of community violence in contemporary society revolves around the events of September 11, 2001. That day shook the security of the nation. United States citizens remember the attacks on the Pentagon and the World Trade Center as the most successful demonstration of terrorism in history. From that day forward, collective death has been felt as political discourse and as a proved media spectacle offered for mass consumption. In the years preceding the attack, the US had lived through multiple wars, such as the Persian Gulf Crisis and the Middle Eastern conflict, and terroristic attacks, such as the first World Trade Center bombing and the Oklahoma City bombing. However, the 9-11 events became the most figural time in memory where the United States had to come to terms with its own sense of being victimized and helpless. Most will remember the horror of the attack and the collective trauma felt by the nation. Natural disasters are no less devastating to communities. Earthquakes, tornadoes, and hurricanes, all resulting from global warming, are increasing. During the writing of this book, for example, a tornado dropped onto an interstate highway, killing eleven and injuring many others. Two weather events – Hurricane Sandy and the Nemo blizzard – had just devastated the northeastern United States. To all such events, the country responded, sometimes in helpful and other times in unhelpful ways. The collective response revealed an interesting truth: The way people experience, perceive, and display distress is culturally determined, and it should be remembered that culture cannot be separated from the worldview of the individual. Culture influences styles of coping.

Because of the short life of news stories, global audiences hold an impression that a few months after a disaster everyone directly involved has recovered and moved on. In terms of grief and loss, most of the literature says that psychological manifestations of these survival patterns do indeed typically resolve on their own within a six-month period following the disastrous event, if homeostatic balance and instrumental need can be restored. The literature on the more complex psychosocial aspects of grief responses to community violence and disaster is extensive. Five survival patterns are noted as typical in the aftermath of such events: (1) death imprint, defined by memories and images of the disaster; (2) death guilt, which is the sense of self-condemnation over having survived while others have died, (3) psychic numbing, noted to be the diminished capacity to feel anything, (4) impaired human relationships, including a conflict over need or nurturance, coupled with suspicion of others, and (5) search for the significance surrounding the disaster, which attempts to provide an explanation for the disaster experience (Lifton & Olson, 1976). The greater the strength of the psychosocial network, the quicker and more effective is neutralization of the loss. The closer the psychological or physical proximity the individual has to the event, the more likely there will be aftershocks and difficulties with grieving the loss. Many people who experience the stress of a disaster will not go on to develop lingering and ongoing symptoms. There is, however, a small percentage that will develop the full complement of symptoms of Post-Traumatic Stress Disorder, which will require more extensive professional intervention.

In the acute period following community violence or disaster, people may experience a greater degree of apathy, including a diminished level of energy and memory capacity, a numbing of emotional feelings toward others, and physical problems. As the community grieves, even positive and constructive relationships become impaired. The need for mutual support remains high, but the process of everyday living becomes burdensome. Personal feelings are easily bruised. Anger and suspicion permeate relationships at a variety of levels. For a period of time, life is generally less than satisfactory. Individuals living through trauma will experience a higher than usual level of arousal, which intensifies reactions to ordinary occurrences. The increased stress can exhaust even the strongest coping mechanisms and leave a person feeling vulnerable. Common reactions include:

- A generalized sense of hopelessness
- Detachment from the event or its impact on others or, alternately, an overly intense sense of despair and desolation
- Difficulty with concentration and decision-making
- Heightened startle response and agitation
- Work and school problems
- Physical reactions including sleep disturbance, gastrointestinal distress, fatigue
- Irritability, outbursts of anger
- Loss of trust of others coupled with a sense of isolation or a desire to withdraw

As people respond in their own idiosyncratic ways, the community tends to wrap its arms around each individual, seeking to find common significance in the meaning of the event or the disaster at a larger level. Even without direct meaning, social convention dictates the creation of ceremonies and memorials. These serve immediate and long-term purposes following a community stressor. The efforts to hold ceremonies facilitate communal mourning and facilitate integration of the loss. Unless the community can find acceptable explanations that give significance and meaning to the event, individuals will be unlikely to be able to find significance and meaning for living on a personal level.

Violence and disaster are public health problems and their effects leave the community vulnerable. Besides being a leading source of injury, they take a toll on more subtle aspects of cognitive, behavioral, social, and emotional functioning. Disruption in any of these psychological domains can affect an individual's progression through the typical and expected developmental steps of life, with the nature of the impact dependent on the timing, type, and chronicity of exposure to the violence or disaster. Because the event typically takes places in a familiar setting, the sense of a "safe haven" is lost and marred by danger and has to be reconciled and integrated.

FAMILY CONFLICT

As author Samira Beckwith writes, "We know how to embrace birth, but our culture seems to have forgotten how to accept death. As a result, the dying process of a loved one is often a very difficult family experience that can test even the closest relationships" (2005, p. 143). Few events affect families more than the death of one of its members. When someone in a family dies, the shock wave is felt throughout the system. The way in which a family construes the loss of its member greatly influences how its members will grieve. Even in families known for mutual support and cohesion, it is not unusual for members to find themselves at odds over virtually any issue associated with the death of their loved one. In the case of one family, the appointed trustee, the oldest son of the deceased, refused to share information about the father's estate before the death. In another case, one sibling had been estranged from the family for years, at least in the others' eyes, though this sibling saw nothing out of place with his relationship to his brothers, sisters, or their deceased father. Even though this sibling had seen his father only "about once a year" for over a decade and had limited contact with his brothers and sisters, he didn't find this to be unusual, and was ready to make plans and be actively involved in estate disposition, much to his siblings' irritation. In a third case, the deceased died intestate, and family members began to fight over possessions before the funeral rites were completed. As one family member said later, "We fought over the blue rug she bought at Wal-Mart. We could've gone to the store and bought one for everybody, but who would've gotten Grandma's? We lost our minds there for a little while."

- Most families simply do not want to discuss death. At the point where there is no avoiding the subject, members involved in such important conversations can feel unprepared and are likely to be emotionally distraught and raw. Decisions such as disposition of estates, funeral arrangements, renegotiation of family roles, and other such matters make for strained communications during tense times. The disruption of individual balance corresponds to shifts in family homeostasis, as one wise young man described, saying, "it knocked the whole family out of whack." (Parris, 2011):The nature of the relationship each member had with the deceased

- The stage of life of both the bereaved and the deceased
- The presence or absence of social support
- The culture in which the bereavement occurs
- The religious or secular background of the bereaved
- The presence of suicide, homicide, or violence
- Sudden death
- The lack of an anticipatory period of adjustment and preparation for the expected death of the family member

Families must be viewed from two perspectives. Each system is a collection of individuals, with grief and response to loss affected by personality, coping abilities, age and maturity, gender, mental and physical health, philosophy of life, fears of or experiences with death, as well as formal and informal supports. Second, the family as a whole has its own personality structure and unique characteristics. This includes the number and personalities of its members, their developmental states, the family's position in the life cycle, interactional patterns, values, norms, and beliefs, equality of relationships, flexibility of communication, coping styles and problem-solving abilities, resources, and strengths. The death of a family member underlines the obvious and latent characteristics, strengths, and vulnerabilities of the family in its entirety.

A story will illustrate. A matriarch of a large family died of natural causes at an advanced age. As her adult children and grandchildren gathered, the minister met them to prepare the eulogy. In ensuing conversations, several of the adult children spoke of their mother's work on behalf of others. "Yeah," said the oldest, "she would take care of others before she'd take care of us. She really wanted to be seen by everyone else as our local Mother Theresa. It isn't how I remember her at all at home." Another sister said, "You really don't want to go there now. She hasn't been dead for 24 hours and here you are – bringing up that old argument that needs to be buried with her." A heated conversation followed.

A second story is also relevant. Another matriarch, living in a small rural community, had seven adult children, all living within a 100-mile radius of the family home. Throughout her long life, whenever asked about her family, she said, "I am the luckiest mother in the world. My children have never had a cross word between them." She died without leaving a will, though there had been informal discussions about "who would get what." Though not a woman of means, as her home was dismantled, family members disagreed over many of the matriarch's possessions. Sons, daughters, and grandchildren "picked sides," and the conflict that had been brewing for years erupted. Looking back, one of the eldest said, "We never did have those 'cross words' in my mother's presence. To have had family fights would've spoiled her story. But you can't live as close as we have for all these years and not step on each other's toes. We were just ripe to argue and say some things that had been festering for years. A fair amount of damage was done, regrettably. If we had been more honest with each other sooner, I don't think things would've been so difficult."

There are other factors that complicate a family's adjustment to the loss of one of its members. At the top of the list, obviously, are existing dysfunctional patterns of family relationships. A death does not change character, it simply highlights it. Where there are difficulties with interactions, communication styles, and problem-solving abilities in a family, a death will heighten and illuminate the deficits. This is also true with the lack of availability or ineffectiveness of formal or informal support systems. Families who are closed, remote, or isolated from others are at high risk for conflict when the system is disturbed by death. Families who experience any type of stigma, whether it is self-imposed or socially sanctioned, can inhibit the family from requesting or receiving needed assistance. This is particularly true when a family lives in poverty and feels oppressed by the lack of social and economic resources.

Grief researcher Therese Rando (1984) suggests several aspects that seem to facilitate a more graceful flow for the family system during the stress of death. Those factors that gird the system's ability to cope more effectively include:

- Knowledge and accurate information related to the cause and circumstances of the death
- Family members' active participation in preparatory care for the deceased at end-of-life, or participation in the funeral rites and rituals following
- Open and honest communication, characterized by some immediacy, allowing for open conversations and discussions related to matters of the deceased, the circumstances of the death, and the feelings associated with the deceased

- Flexible family structures that allow members to adjust and re-adjust to the changing role structure that results from the loss
- Positive relationships among family members that allow for differences and encourage compatible problem-solving strategies
- Availability of effective informal and formal support systems
- Social and economic resources and the absence of concurrent family problems and crises, all of which combine to maximize effective coping
- A philosophical or religious belief system that allows for a sense of continuity for the family, including a hopeful interpretive framework for the loss

Families are unique in their presentation of a personality. Just as no two individuals will respond in exactly the same ways to a loss, no two families will deal the same way with the impact of a death in the system. There is no doubt of the psychological truth that the impact of a death makes the system more vulnerable for a while. The task for the family is to discover and utilize its strengths to compensate for its systemic frailties during a stressful time. This occurs through facilitation of communication between family members, including those who were intimate caregivers of the deceased and those who were less engaged but still connected and invested in the system's continuity. Discussion of realistic and observable options related to the "next steps" of the family can lower barriers and identify strategies that may take the edge off of the tension that is bound to be present.

Although discussed in an earlier chapter, another case must be made for advance directives. Because of the changes in healthcare and the politicalization of the costs of end-of-life care, there is growing interest in advanced directives as a means of enabling families' avoidance of disputes in the early stages of grief following loss. All individuals should have advance directives, which is the general term referring to a person's instructions about future medical care in the event that the individual becomes unable to communicate. These healthcare directions should be as important to the family as they are to the individual. The process of creating and documenting advance directives provides, by design, open and ongoing communication among family members and medical professionals. Without advance directives, conflict can arise which can lead to family distress that could otherwise have been prevented. While advance directives may not be fully adequate in some instances, particularly where there is more entrenched family pathology, they do offer an opportunity for more open and healthy communication among family members.

X

Healing, Meaning-Making, and the Myth of Closure

You will learn how to fly and God will give you a safe place to land.

Frederick Nietzsche

To everything there is a season, a time to be born and a time to die.

Ecclesiastes 3:1

Death changes the psychological, social, and family landscape of an individual. One who survives the death of a loved one adapts to a life requiring the confrontation of the painfully real absence of the physical being of the loved one. A new orientation is required to adapt and orient to a world that at least for a time, is strange because of the loss. Energetic transitions are demanded as the individual moves toward a new, and in many ways, unknown future.

THE MYTH OF CLOSURE

In the world of life and loss, contemporary understandings have changed the definitions of the endpoint of grief work. Historically, grief was a finite process, marked by closure, when the survivor had thoroughly detached from the deceased and "moved on" to new relationships. Elisabeth Kübler-Ross's original work on grief was misinterpreted as a linear stage theory quickly after it was introduced into the western zeitgeist. This misrepresentation of the grief process produced the belief that grief has a demarcated end, and that it is emotionally healthier to close the door on loss than it is to live with it. In the myth, those who do their grief work effectively are assumed to find some finality in the process. If the individual is "normal," then a psychological period must be placed at the end of the sentence. It is now recognized that closure is indeed a myth, and integration is a much more valid and elegant 'endpoint' for the resolution of loss. When a death occurs, life rhythms and meanings are ruptured, relationships go awry, and families are at increased risk of conflict. Those grieving will typically look for points of certainty, but a concrete sense of loss is always elusive. In truth, searching for closure is essentially a death-denying mechanism and a way of "stiff-arming" the experience of grief from authentic contact. Grief demands understanding, brought about through reflection on the personal experience of loss. For a time following the loss, the desperate search for meaning is replaced with unrelenting confusion; the mind seeks to make sense of the nonsensical. Grief begins with loss. By definition, it holds an incomplete emptiness characterized by yearning and pain as the search ensues for a realization of the changes exacted by the death. The only way to find healing is through resilience and the search for meaning. Grief allows people the freedom to remember the lost person and move forward, full of hope and in the presence of new relationships.

Grief is not an illness. It is an expected and typical reaction to loss, and for the most part, should not be pathologized. As grief researcher Pauline Boss says, "…it manifests itself physically (tears, somatic symptoms, lack of sleep, change in appetite), psychologically (sadness, anger, denial, ambivalence), and socially (loss of identity, loss of attachment, loss of trust in the world as a safe place)" (2012, p. 462). In an interesting paradox, the lack of closure allows for new avenues of exploration, experimentation, and creativity. This paradox assumes that an individual will embrace the pain associated with the loss, and work with it until malleable. Those who mourn learn that paradoxical thinking helps soothe pain; they begin to appreciate that truth is relative, context driven, and that contradictions abound. As a widow talked about her deceased husband, she said, "I am married and not married. He is dead, but in many ways, he's more alive than he's ever been to me. I think about him and our life together every minute of the day. I am a walking contradiction: There are times that I feel alive, times that I feel dead, and times I wish I would die. I can't think about 'the facts of life' anymore. I just have to listen to what rings true, and know that it'll probably be different tomorrow."

Cultural differences in how, when, and where to grieve, as well as the impact of different types of loss prohibit a standard "how-to" prescription for grieving. Rather than a prescribed template, those who mourn need human connection, "…along with society's empathy, compassion, and patience" (Boss, 2012, p. 462). There is a rich body of literature clarifying that cultural traditions, beliefs, and values make a difference in how people outwardly express their grief and how they try to cope with it. Specific bereavement practices vary depending on the cultural and ethnic background of those in the situation, and failure to follow through with particular traditional practices or rituals after the death can have a devastating impact on the individual and family. No cultural practice endorses closure. Instead, bereavement is noted to take place within the context of families and communities and is played out in endless varieties of social interactions. Cultural diversity embraces the differences among people based on a shared ideology and a valued set of beliefs, norms, customs, and meanings evidenced in a way of life. As an undergraduate psychology student summed up the discussion, "Culture counts."

There is no doubt of a connection among culture, grief, and bereavement. There are habits of mind and sentiments of heart that are the product of growing up in a particular culture. Different cultures provide lenses through which reality is viewed. Therefore, great relevance is given to the idea of avoiding blanket generalizations about any specific group. Assuming that all individual members of a certain culture think, believe, and behave exactly alike is apt to result in stereotyping and insensitive contact and care. As part of the process of being culturally astute, heightened attention and curiosity towards the person's grieving process remains crucial. To fully understand another's cultural perspective, those who grieve must be invited to identify their experience and teach others about their perspective on that experience. An anthropologist noted, "Humans are emotional beings with different experiences. The way people express themselves is different, and what moves one person may not even touch another. It is the state of mind, which is influenced by the culture." This speaks to the notion that human perceptions matter significantly, because they are real in their consequences. In general, it should also be remembered that, during the acute stage of the grieving process, the deceased continues to be related to mourners in active and "living" ways. The goal of grief is to help the survivor to move the deceased to "living memory" that can be relied on during times of personal crisis and success as a source of comfort and compassion.

All in all, time lines for closure are unrealistic and often times culturally biased. Regrettably, Western culture seems to insist on a linear progression of grief, and without this artificial sense of closure, a grieving individual is erroneously pathologized. The case has been made that closure is a false goal in conversations about life and loss. While still popular, the stage theory of grief is simply wrong: Time lines for closure are unrealistic and culturally biased. Even after the certainty of death, a relationship continues on many levels through remembrance, traditions, and symbols of affection. The integration of a loved one into memory is the absolute expected outcome of grief.

RESILIENCE

Resilience is best defined as the outcome of successful adaptation to adversity. It is "the ability of adults in otherwise normal circumstances, who are exposed to an isolated and potentially disruptive event, such as the death of a close relation or a violent of life-threatening situation, to maintain relatively stable, healthy levels of psychological and physical functioning, as well as the capacity for generative experiences and positive emotions" (Bonanno, 2004, p. 260). A more familiar description of resilience is found in its characterization of an individual's ability to "bounce," as in "bounce back" and recover from challenges of daily living. People who are resilient display a reliable capacity to quickly regain equilibrium physiologically, psychologically, socially, and interpersonally following stressful events. They are able to sustain this sense of bounce and continue to move forward in the face of adversity. Though resilience is nearly universal to all, people vary in their capacities to manifest inner strength, flexibility, and reserve. Attention to social and contextual factors is needed since the responsiveness of the social and physical environment differs from one family to another and from one community to the next. The range of reactions that people exhibit when confronted with interpersonal loss is wide.

Of particular interest is whether individuals are likely to be resilient when faced with a loss. The experience of loss is an integral and challenging part of human development. It is a regrettable truth that most people will be exposed to loss or potentially traumatic events during their lifetime. Almost everyone is likely to experience the pain and disorientation resulting from the death of a loved one. The stress of the experience taxes even the hardiest individual, and can undermine feelings of safety and the sense of justice and fairness. However, there is a growing awareness that the majority of people can endure the stress of death without experiencing damaging disruptions in functioning. Even when faced with the most highly aversive events, "…many, if not most people demonstrate genuine resilience to their deleterious effects" (Mancini & Bonanno, 2006, p. 973). Resilience is a complex phenomenon, resulting from a mix of factors including personality, supportive relationships, and the type, severity, and duration of the stressor. While most people possess capacities that are globally associated with resilience, whether they actually call on and use them can only be determined in terms of the outcome after the event. The key seems to be found in the pattern of recovery, characterized by adaption in the context of adversity.

The researcher, S.E. Hobfoll (1998), has developed a theory called conservation of resource. He hypothesizes that loss of any kind of resource that is valued by the individual triggers a stress reaction, since the individual – by nature – generally strives for maintenance or improvement of personal resource. The theory continues, saying that an individual will look to limit the loss by mobilizing remaining resources in an attempt to mitigate the adverse effects of the loss. Based on this general definition, resilient individuals are less affected by resource loss, or are able to limit the impact of resource loss. It should be noted that many of the great grief researchers, while subscribing to Hobfoll's theory, diverge in their opinion of whether resilience includes recovery and growth processes, or is just characterized by the sense of 'bounce' back to baseline. The prevailing school of thought defines resilience by the ability to maintain a stable equilibrium, which reflects the individual's capacity of stress resistance. This attribute is seen as different from recovery, which has a different trajectory of adaptation. As Boener and Jopp (2010) note,

> Whereas resilience can involve some initial distress following a loss, the dominant pattern is a relatively stable, positive emotional state before and after the loss, without any substantial downward peaks. In contrast, the pattern of recovery typically involves a clearly identifiable time of "not doing well" in response to loss, which is then followed by recovery or a return to 'normal.' The key idea for this latter notion of resilience is the ability to bounce back from setbacks in life. In a more integrative manner…recovery [is seen] as a special case of resilience and suggests viewing resilience as a family of loosely connected phenomena involving adequate or better adaptation in the context of adversity. (p. 128)

There are multiple predictors that can be employed when considering an individual's capacity for mustering resilience in the face of death or loss. The cause of death and the circumstances surrounding it are generally considered as important indicators of bereavement outcomes. Resilience is unlikely if the death of a loved one was sudden or violent. It is also questionable whether an individual can bounce back from death following a lengthy illness where the bereaved was the primary caregiver (even though most caregivers report relief and a significant reduction of stress after the death). The type and quality of relationship held with the deceased are also noted as important variables in the likelihood of an individual's resilience. For couples, resilience seems more likely between partners who are positively connected but not overly dependent on each other. Older adults who lose a spouse or partner generally manifest more resilience than younger adults. Empirical findings show that women are more likely to be resilient when their husbands die. At the same time, resilience is less often observed in women who lose a child. It is speculated, though, that these findings might be related to gender roles rather than to gender itself. In the context of loss, mental and physical health seem to be important to resilience. Personality factors have been addressed in various studies on bereavement, but overall, evaluations of an individual's character has been less useful in predicting grief trajectories when compared to other mental health variables. There is evidence, though, to suggest that resilient individuals tend to be more extroverted and have lower levels of neuroticism. They are prone to be more optimistic and indicate higher levels of happiness.

Finding resilience in no way eliminates stress and pain. The volatility of grief is always present following a loss. The road to resilience lies in working with emotions, thoughts, and perspectives that cause distress. Individuals can improve their capacity for resilience at any time of life. It develops with maturity and experience with flexible thinking, self-management skills, and the exercise of options and choices. It also comes from supportive relationships with significant others. Resilience is also culturally based in ethnic, religious, and regional traditions. The compliment of resilient behaviors, thoughts, and actions can be learned and developed across the life span. In summary, factors that contribute to resilience include:

- close relationships with family and friends
- a positive view of self and a sense of being "in charge"
- personal confidence and accurate self-appraisal of strengths and abilities
- the ability to manage strong feelings and impulses
- good problem-solving and communication skills
- the ability to seek help and resources
- the ability to help others, even when in distress
- the attribution of positive meaning to difficult events

MAKING MEANING FROM GRIEF

Victor Frankl's work, *Man's Search for Meaning* (1962) speaks to the sense that people are driven by the psychological need to find or create a sense of meaning and purpose in their lives, and that this drive facilitates the personal capacity to face and transcend even the most horrible experiences. His theme can be applied to different types of experience of human suffering, including grief and bereavement. Those who survive the loss of a loved one must adapt to a life marked by the painfully real absence of the deceased, so meaning-making becomes particularly important when individuals are dealing with losses due to death. By its nature, loss due to death is not directly amenable to problem-solving as a way out of the situation. Instead, individuals must find a means to come to terms with the loss via intrapsychic, internal processes. Survivors find a new orientation to a world that is made strange by the loss, in a way that calls for practical, psychological, social, and spiritual transitions, all while moving toward an unknown future. Living through the death of a significant other is an event that can validate or invalidate the beliefs that form the basis of the survivor's life. The grief that follows loss is an intensely personal process, one that is idiosyncratic, intimate, and inextricable from the felt sense of "this is who I am." In addition to surrendering to the pain of the loss, grief creates a need to process the loss of psychological balance and adjust to a changed life brought about by the death. Those living with grief must reestablish a life that feels worthy of passionate reinvestment. The question arises: How does a person navigate the pathways through loss? The answer is found in actions that affirm or reconstruct a personal world of meaning that has been challenged by the loss.

Meaning-making is a process of re-creating schemas and representations of the self in the world, so that the feeling of order and coherence is reestablished. These representations constitute a perspective that an individual carries defining the world, the self, personal aspirational goals, and relevant life events marking the process toward these goals. In order to recover from a distressing and disruptive life event, such as the death of a loved one, the individual initiates, on both conscious and unconscious levels, a search for meaning. This search takes place personally and communally, since meaning is just as strongly connected to cultural values, beliefs, and the social context in which the meaning-making takes place, as it is to the intrapsychic sense of self.

Psychologists describe this sense of making and remaking meaning from events as coming from a *constructivist* perspective. Human beings are seen as self-organizing and self-regulating, holding the ability to punctuate the flow of experience into significant episodes. These episodes are organized in the mind in patterns, much like a book's chapters, so that the individual can anticipate, interpret, and negotiate complicated and complex life challenges in a lively, workable fashion. The death of a significant other threatens this capacity, since it can invalidate the survivor's sense of secure grounding. As one young fellow said, "Before my mother died, life made sense. Now, it doesn't." His task becomes that of working to reaffirm and reconstruct the world of meaning that has been disrupted by the loss. The young man continued, "I still feel like I need to turn to her to ask questions. But she's gone. When I need her to be present the most is when I feel her absence in such an awful way. It is a strange experience to be motherless."

This constructivist approach supports the notion that the landscape of loss is dynamic and changing, all dependent on the central issues of meaning of re-balancing and recovering from significant loss. The framework of this process is fairly simple and approachable. Individuals have a set of basic beliefs and goals that set the course for a sense of purpose or meaning in life. These are what individuals typically believe about the world and the goals toward which they are oriented. Theorists call this a global meaning system. When confronted with any potential stressor, the person assigns meaning to the event, which provides definition and clarity. This is known as appraised meaning. The individual experiences discomfort and distress to the extent that the appraised meaning is discrepant and at odds with global meaning. Following loss, a shattering of assumptions violates global beliefs. Such distress in turn initiates new meaning-making efforts to bring global and appraised meanings closer to each other (assimilation)or, at times, to change global meaning (accommodation). The goal of meaning-making is to reduce discrepancies between situational and global meaning, which will lead to better adjustment. Therefore, grieving becomes an act of affirming or reconstructing a personal world of meaning that has been challenged by loss. Adaptation to loss involves restoration of coherence to the narrative of life.

The term "coping" is commonly used when an individual describes the grieving process. (In the Southern vernacular of the United States, this is translated into, "How's she taking it?") There is a lack of consensus, though, that coping and meaning-making are synonymous. Coping is seen as the cognitive and behavioral efforts to overcome internal and external demands and the conflicts between them that are evaluated as exceeding personal resources. These efforts come in two directions: There can be problem-solving strategies, aimed at changing the relationship between the person and environment, or cognitive reframing, which aims to change the way the relationship is interpreted. The emotional component of coping depends on the individual's potential and future expectations, i.e., whether grief recovery will be associated with hope or hopelessness. Coping is dependent on the individual's level of social risk and feeling of vulnerability. A woman described this sense: "After my child died, I felt like I was skinned alive. I was completely raw and didn't want to be touched by anyone, including those people that I knew who loved me. I couldn't even hold myself for a while. During that time, I never felt like I would be normal again. I just felt like I was damaged beyond repair. The world went on around me. I didn't try to avoid anything in particular; it all just seemed to work around me. Eventually, I would get a glimpse of something that felt good, and I held onto these soothing moments like a talisman. I would've never guessed that I could grow new skin. But I did. Now, don't get me wrong: There is a part of me that will always be raw and fragile as I remember my son, but I can manage now and know that there is life for me, even in the presence of his death. I've always liked good drama – theater, television, books, you name it. In good writing, there is always a 'back story.' That's the place that my child's death now holds for me. It is a part of my back story – a significant part of who I am, but not who I lead with."

This exquisite example provides a glimpse into the woman's process of grief, meaning-making, and the insight gained from her grief. Insight is a necessary component of meaning-making, and is defined as a new perspective about self or others. Insight varies in terms of content, making new links between the past and present, or, as illustrated above, between conscious thought and the underlying schema that guides behavior. When the metaphorical light bulb pops on in a person's mind, there is a conscious and clear shift of meaning that involves new connections. The woman's metaphor of the 'back story' gave her some sense of cause and effect, of a feeling and understanding that 'this-relates-to-that.' Insight provides rich and accessible definition to integration and has a sense of salience and relevance to the individual's conception of self. As the woman above said, "That's the place that my child's death now holds for me." The insight came to her gradually and now stays near to her consciousness.

Insight and understanding are synonymous. Both are defined by new meaning. An old Appalachian mountain woman described it this way: "I stood under my grief for several years after my husband died. I had two children to raise and was lucky enough to sign on at the post office. But I just went through the motions of work for the longest time. The only thing that I really enjoyed was found in my relationship with my boys. After a time, though, I came out from under the grief, and began to see the world in a new and different light. It happened over time, and I realized that I had more OK days than I had hard ones. Looking back, I was working things out, without even knowing that I was working them out." Insight is different from awareness, though, which does not involve new connections or causality. Instead, it holds newness and a level of conscious awareness that builds on self-knowledge. For most, insight contains an element of hindsight, where a person can look back and construct meaning from the lived experience.

To develop insight, a grieving individual must be open to experience. For those who are in more of a reactive mode to the loss, meaning-making remains at arm's length. A sense of self-awareness is necessary to the process, such that an individual might say, "Well, look at me." As a man said, "I am along for the ride. Ever since the death of my friend, I keep going into unknown territory. I figure I can either fight it or go with it. Either way, I'm going to be riding. So I might as well see the territory." This sense of reflexivity is likely to serve him well, since he moves into new experience with his eyes wide open. There are psychic energies that facilitate the process. Feeling creative and motivated helps the flow of insight. Another fellow described this, saying, "I keep looking for meaning, for understanding, for anything that can help me get a grip on all that I lost. The death is just the most obvious. Since there is nothing tangible to hold onto anymore, I figure it has to be spiritual. I guess people will think that I'm crazy, but I talk this through. I appreciate those who will listen, and just disregard those who don't."

Social support does help bring insight. By its nature, insight is difficult to develop in isolation. Reliable feedback from others about one's own process and impact develops the higher level of functioning that allows for seeing what is beyond conscious sight. As the man above reported, belief that insight is attainable, with the support of others who believe that insight is desirable and necessary for change lends empathy and compassion to the period of exploration leading to the newness of the "aha!" that insight brings. The man continued, "The way I have this figured is that my head thinks and my heart feels. They have two different jobs. What connects my head and my heart is my neck, and that's where my vocal cords are. So, talking has to make them work together, right? When I can talk things through with someone I trust, I feel like I can make sense out of what I feel, and then both head and heart seem right."

So how does insight facilitate grief recovery? Initially, it changes symptoms. When insight is anticipated, there is a sense of movement and motion. A grieving woman reported that, "…the most awful place that I find myself is when I'm stuck. I hate the sense of being stagnant and moldy more than any other." The fluid nature of insight mollifies stress and encourages a general sense of what is positive. The woman continued, saying, "After some months following my partner's death, I started seeing my life as a puzzle that I couldn't put together. I could identify that it was a puzzle, but couldn't see how it could work out. What I realized, though, is that I had a strong desire to understand the puzzle, so I started reading, talking, thinking. I was wandering through my life, my partner's life, our time together, and how I had changed as a result. It was a more emotional time, wandering like this, than it was right after the death, but my tears felt cleansing rather than agonizing. My memories seemed more like clues than problems."

So, insight serves as preparation for a change in behavior, and allows the individual to make difficult decisions. The woman continued, "At one point along the way, I realized that I didn't need such a big house. My children were not ready for me to sell the home place, but I needed a new space. It was sad to sell the house we had shared, but I was so involved with the process and this seemed so right as I moved along with it. I told others that I was 'travelling light,' and that they should wish me well."

Insight increases what social workers call an individual's *agency*, rather than referring to the external world of *structure*. Agency refers to the capacity of individuals to act independently and to make their own free choices. By contrast, structures are those factors of influence (such as social class, religion, gender, ethnicity, customs, etc.) that determine or limit an agent's decisions. An individual's agency is clearly based on the independent capability or ability to act with autonomy and free will. This ability is affected by the cognitive belief structure which has been formed through experience, the perceptions held by the society and the individual, and the structures and circumstances of the environment one is in. Insight and agency help the individual to hold paradox without frustration, but instead with the expectation that the conflict will lead to something creative.

HEALING AND RELEARNING THE WORLD

Grief ushers in change and the process of relearning a complex world. It involves finding obvious, hidden, and metaphorical meanings that are then applied on many levels in contemporary life. Grief occurs individually and collectively in complicated interdependent interactions with family, friends, and community. Essentially, grief allows a person to make the transition from "…loving in presence to loving in absence. And we reweave that lasting love into the larger, richly complex fabric of our lives" (Attig, 2001, p. 34).

Healing occurs as life is put back together following the death of a loved one. A new shape, with new integrity, emerges in daily living. There is a renewed sense of continuity and meaning in the personal stories of everyday life. This process is accomplished through the struggle to come to terms with the pain and anguish accompanying the devastation and deconstruction caused by the death and the hard labor of grieving itself. As healing proceeds, pain either dissipates or the survivor learns to carry it without encumbrance. As Thomas Attig (2001) says, "We move from being our pain – being wholly absorbed in it and preoccupied with it – to having our pain – to carrying residual sadness and heartache in our hearts. We carry it in a place alongside other places where we hold those who died in lasting love and where we love others, love ourselves, and hold the cares that give our lives meaning and bring us joy and fulfillment. We find and give meaning to our suffering" (p. 34).

Healing manifests in new definitions of self in terms of character, history and roles, and the identities found within them. Practice must come along with the newness, which builds new strategies for coping and esteem. As one man said, "My wife was sick for a very long time. While we had caregivers for her, I took on more and more of the home-and-hearth tasks. I learned how to wash clothes, cook, clean, and manage the household. I had fancied myself as a twentieth century guy who had 'helped out' with these tasks while we were raising our children. I learned differently through the care giving experience that I couldn't just help out. I was chief, cook, and bottle washer. Since she died, I realized what a gift all of that was. I can take care of myself now pretty effectively. Before all of this, I would've made jokes about my masculinity. Now, I just see it all as a part of what I need to do to live in the world with some degree of health and social propriety. Some might call me a new man. I believe that I'm the same guy, just with new and improved skills."

The relearning and meaning-making the man speaks to is more than taking in information and mastering new ideas. It is more of a matter of learning how to be and act in the world, literally without those we love by our sides. Healing occurs through the transformation of habits, motivations, dispositions, and general ways of doing things. As the man said, there is a blend of old and new ways of meeting personal need. In grief, little can be taken for granted. Self-conscious reflection of old habits, patterns, traditions, "tried-and-trues," and "taken-for-granteds" are no longer viable because they require the presence of the one who has died. Grief takes the survivor into deliberate examination of alternative courses, and new meaning is created out of the experimentation.

As the man in the earlier example learned, the meaning that was found in his daily life may not have occurred had he not suffered the loss of his wife. Grief gives no choice about what happened. However, human nature allows for the individual to grow positively through the experience. Again, as Tom Attig (2001) writes, "We find new strength of character. We grow in self-understanding and self-esteem. We become more sensitive and responsive to others. We learn how much others mean to us and learn new ways to show appreciation and love. We gain new critical perspectives on our relationships, our reality, and on the human condition" (p. 43).

When focus is placed on finding meaning, grief shifts. Finding meaning requires holding multiple truths about the deceased, the survivor, and the relationship held between the two. The remembering is akin to exercising a broken arm back to use following an accident. In the wake of loss, some good things come. Another young man, who grieved mightily after his father's sudden death, reflected on his experience, saying, "It was like I washed up on the beach after having nearly drowned. It took me a while to recover, but then I realized I was no longer at sea, and was able to get my legs back and move on." A lovely research study by Frantz, Farrell, and Trolley (2001), bears witness to the young man's truth: Significant, positive things do result for an overwhelming majority of grieving people. The researchers asked people who had lost a loved one to death approximately a year earlier about what good things had come of it, what they had learned as a result, and how they were different. Four major positive themes emerged:

1. Many bereaved people said they learned to appreciate the value of life more than they ever did before. They reported more experience with living in the moment, regularly re-examining priorities, and placing greater importance on spending time with family, friends, and loved ones.

2. They reported becoming stronger as a result of surviving the pain of death and learning how to step forward to handle things that previously were done by the deceased person. Many said they were more independent, mature, self-reliant, and self-confident, much to their own surprise, and had newfound and unexpected strength.

3. Many found themselves much closer to their loved ones and family than before the death. Even for those who were not, the theme of "not taking others for granted" resonated for most.

4. Most said they had done things to help themselves that worked and made at least some positive difference in coping with their loss. In an interesting paradox, the ones who reported the most successful coping would find times to feel the pain of the loss and, at other times, find ways not to do so. They embraced and avoided grief at the same time.

It should be noted that there was a small, but noticeable, group of people who reported they were significantly worse after the death. They felt devastated by the loss and moved into loneliness and isolation. They reported a sense of resignation after the death, and feeling helpless, hard, and colder than before. While such reactions are not unusual in earlier parts of the grieving process, they often diminish over time, but not for everyone.

Healing and meaning-making are self-referential, relational, and exist in a dynamic sense of dialogue. The narrative that the individual tells is a work in progress. Meaning-making is constructed through language, not only what is told, but how it is told. The healing and narrative must be understood in retrospect. As one man said, "I finally understood my grief from a broader perspective." In many ways, meaning-making is a remembrance, fashioned by the storyteller. Another man described his experience, saying, "I think I'm in the middle of my story. I can't be sure how it will end. After my wife's death, I've had to revise the plot, and expect I'll have to do more of this as new events are added to my life. I have learned that I'm more than my history, which is a good thing. I'm definitely a work in progress and I anticipate what I might be."

ACCOMMODATING TO THE MYSTERY

An old story related to life and loss has been told: News was brought to the rabbi that his friend in the neighboring town had fallen ill and died. On the Sabbath, he said her name over and over and prayed for her soul and for the healing of her kin. Then he put on new shoes of the finest leather, laced them up tight, called the congregation, and they danced. A member of the congregation who was present said: "Power flowed forth from the dancing. Every step was powerful mystery. An unfamiliar light suffused the house, and everyone watching saw the heavenly host join in the dance."

Grief, healing, and recovering from loss is found in the presence of death, which is one of the great mysteries of life and the human condition. When those who are loved die, survivors wonder and search for meaning, order, and understanding within the greater scheme of things. Those who grieve draw on, seek, explore, and ponder about understandings, perspectives, and experiences that can ground confidence in what is beyond rational thought. The struggle to accept and come to terms with the great mysteries of finiteness, change, imperfection, uncertainty, and vulnerability ensues. Death challenges people in ways that ordinary problems do not.

The experiences of life and loss are constants. They are provocative, too important to ignore and present themselves in dynamic, constantly changing perspectives. Grief is a difficult challenge, and the death of a loved one commands attention. A lovely woman described her grief experience, saying, "All of a sudden, my sense of permanence was gone. I found that I had a lot less control of things than I thought I did. I felt every one of my flaws and kept falling short of things I felt like I absolutely had to do. My knowledge was limited and my judgment questionable. Funny thing, though. As I came to terms with my husband's death, I found that things stayed temporary, and I began to like the feeling of tentativeness in life's journey. I began to read poetry again and saw meaning with fresh eyes. I held people and their relationships with me in new ways. Sometimes I am satisfied, sometimes I'm not. What I do know is that each encounter calls on me to think about myself in challenging ways. I've learned that I cannot control or solve every problem at once, answer all questions definitely, or master every uncertainty. And that's OK."

As heard above, coming to terms with the mystery of death through meaning-making is tentative, at best. Meanings are found within personal histories and surrounding cultures, families, and communities. Over time, and with healing, the greater scheme of life becomes more acceptable to the ones who grieve and mourn. The lesson is learned that love does not die with the physical absence of the deceased. Instead, a new presence for the memory of the deceased is given to the survivor's life. New threads of caring are rewoven and blended into life histories that are shaped and redirected over time and through experiences. These changes then join with enduring connections and are again made whole in personal, familial, and communal ways. The deceased is ascribed a place in the larger context of the survivor's sense of self.

Grieving is a journey of the heart that brings the fullness of life into the here-and-now. The mystery is beautifully described in Dag Hammarskjold's entry in his diary, *Markings*. Hammarskjold was a former UN Secretary General who kept the diary, begun when he was 20 years old, and ending at his death in 1961, in a plane crash in Africa. The entry is as follows:

Is it a new country, in another world of reality Than Days?

Or did I live there before day was?

I awoke to an ordinary morning with grey light reflected in the street,

But still remembered the dark-blue night above the tree line,

The open moor in moonlight, the crest in shadow,

Remembered other dreams of the same mountain country:

Twice I stood on its summits

I stayed by its remotest lake,
And followed the river toward its source.
The seasons have changed
And the light, and the weather, and the hour.
But it is the same land
And I begin to know the map
And to get my bearings.

References

Agency for Healthcare Research and Quality. (2003). *Advance care planning: Preferences for care at the end of life*. Retrieved from www.ahrq.gov/research/endliferia/endria.htm.

American College of Physicians. (2005). Ethics manual. *Annals of Internal Medicine*. Retrieved from http://www.acponline.org/running_practice/ethics/naual/ethicman5th.htm

American Psychiatric Association. (2012). *Proposed revision for adjustment disorder*. Retrieved from http://www.dsm5.org/Proposed-Revision/Pages/proposedrevision.aspx?rid=367#

American Psychiatric Association. (2000). *Diagnostic and statistical manual of mental disorders* (4th ed., text rev.). Washington, DC: Author.

American Association of Suicidology. (n.d.). *Suicide in the U.S.A. based on current (2007) statistics*. Retrieved from http://www.suicidology.org/c/document_library/get_file?folderId=248&name=DLFE-415.pdf

Archer, J. (2008). Theories of grief: Past, present, and future perspectives. In M.S. Stroebe, R.O. Hansson, H. Schut, & W. Stroebe (Eds.), *Handbook of bereavement research and practice* (pp. 45-61). Washington, DC: American Psychological Association.

Arnold, J., & Gemma, P.B. (2008). The continuing process of parental grief. *Death Studies, 32*, 658-673.

Attig, T. (2001). Relearning the world: Making and finding meanings. In R. Neimeyer (Ed.). (2001). *Meaning reconstruction and the experience of loss* (pp. 33-53). Washington, DC: American Psychological Association.

Battin, M.P. (1994). Applied professional ethics and organized religion. *Professional Ethics: A Multidisciplinary Journal, 3*(2), 5-15.

Beckwith, S.K. (2005). When families disagree: Family conflict and decisions. In K.J. Doka, B. Jennings, & C. Corr (Eds). (2005). *Ethical dilemmas at the end of life* (pp. 143-156). Washington, DC: Hospice Foundation of America.

Blauner, R. (1966). Death and social structure. *Psychiatry, 29*, 378-394.

Borkovec, T.D. & Inz, J. (1990). The nature of worry in generalized anxiety disorder: A predominance of thought activity. *Behaviour Research and Therapy, 27*, 263-268.

Boss, P. & Carnes, D. (2012). The myth of closure. *Family Process, 51*(4), 456-469.

Boss, P. (1999). *Ambiguous loss: Learning to live with unresolved grief.* Cambridge, MA: Harvard University Press.

Bowlby, J. (1969). *Attachment and loss: Loss, sadness and depression* (Vol. 3). New York, NY: Basic Books.

Bowlby, J. (1988). *A secure base: Clinical applications of attachment theory.* London, England: Routledge.

Brooks, D. (2011). *The social animal: The hidden sources of love, character, and achievement.* New York, NY: Random House.

Bugental, J.F.T. & Bugental, E.K. (1984). A fate worse than death: The fear of changing. *Psychotherapy, 21*, 543-549.

Campos, J.J., Barrett, K., Lamb, M.E., Goldsmith, H.H., & Sternberg, C. (1939). Socioemotional development. In M.M. Haith & J.J. Campos (Eds.), *Handbook of child psychology: Infancy and developmental psychobiology* (4th ed., Vol. 2, pp. 783-915). New York, NY: Wiley.

Centers for Disease Control, National Center for Health Services. (2005). *Deaths, percent of total deaths, and death rates for the 15 leading causes of death: United States and each state, 2005.* Retrieved from http://www.cdc.gov/nchs/data/dvs/LCWK9_2005.pdf

Chinman, M., Kloos, B., O'Connell, M., & Davidson, L. (2002). Service providers' views of psychiatric mutual support groups. *Journal of Community Psychology, 30*, 349-366.

Corless, I.B. (1986). Spirituality for whom? In F. S. Wald (Ed.), *In search of the spiritual component of hospice care* (pp. 175-191). New Haven, CT: Yale Press.

Cullinan, A. (1993). Bereavement and the sacred art of spiritual care. In K.J. Doka & J.D. Morgan (Eds.), *Death and spirituality* (pp. 195-205). Amityville, NY: Baywood Publishing.

Culver, C.M. (1998). Advance directives. *Psychology: Public, Policy, and Law, 4*(3), 676-687.

DeSpelder, L.A. & Strickland, A.L. (1999). *The last dance: Encountering death and dying* (5th ed.). Mountain View, CA: Mayfield Publishing.

Didion, J. (2005). *The year of magical thinking.* New York, NY: Alfred A. Knopf.

Ellerhorhost-Ryan, J. (1985). Selecting an instrument to measure spiritual distress. *Oncology Nurse Forum, 12*(2), 93-99.

Eliot, T.S. (1936). *Selected writings.* New York, NY: Winggold Press.

Feifel, H. (1990). Psychology and death: Meaningful rediscovery. In L.A. DeSpelder & A.L. Strickland (Eds.). *American Psychologist, 45,* 19-28.

Fraley, R.C. & Shaver, P.R. (1999). Loss and bereavement: Attachment theory and recent controversies concerning "grief work" and the nature of detachment. In J. Cassidy & P.R. Shaver (Eds.), *Handbook of attachment: Theory, research, and clinical applications* (pp. 735-759). New York, NY: Guilford Press.

Frankl, V. (1962). *Man's search for meaning.* New York: Touchstone Books.

Frantz, T.T., Farrell, M.M., & Trolley, B.C. (2001). Positive outcomes of losing a loved one. In R. Neimeyer (Ed.). *Meaning reconstruction and the experience of loss* (pp.191-209). Washington, DC: American Psychological Association.

Freud, S. (1957). Mourning and melancholia (J. Strachey, Trans.). In J. Strachey (Ed.), *The standard edition of the complete psychological works of Sigmund Freud* (Vol. 14, pp. 239-260). London, England: Hogarth Press and Institute of Psychoanalysis.

Garrett, T.M., Baillie, H.W., & Garrett, R.M. (2010). *Health care ethics: Principles and problems* (5th ed.). Boston, MA: Prentice-Hall.

Gendler, R. (1984). *The book of qualities.* New York, NY: Harper Perennial.

Gilbert, R.B. (2006). When adult children grieve the death of a parent: Spiritual perspectives. *The Forum, 32*(2), 10-122.

Grobstein, P. (2003). *Making the unconscious conscious and vice versa: A bi-directional bridge between neuroscience/cognitive science and psychotherapy?* Retrieved from http://serendip.brynmawr.edu/sci_cult/mentalhealth/uncon.html

Hammarskjold, D. (1963). *Markings.* New York: Ballantine Books.

Hiebert, P.G. (2009). *Transforming worldviews: An anthropological understanding of how people change.* Grand Rapids, MI: Baker Press.

Irving, J. (1989). *A prayer for Owen Meany.* New York, NY: William Morrow.

Kass, L.R. (1971). Death as an event: A commentary on Robert Morrison. *Science, 173,* 698-702.

Kastenbaum, R. (2008). Grieving in contemporary society. In M.S. Stroebe, R.O. Hansson, W. Stroebe, & H. Schut (Eds.), *Handbook of bereavement research: Consequences, coping, and care* (pp. 67-85). Washington, DC: American Psychological Association.

Kastenbaum, R. (1977). *Death, society, and human experience.* New York, NY: Mosby.

Keesee, N.J., Currier, J.M., & Neimeyer, R.A. (2008). Predictors of grief following the death of one's child: The contribution of finding meaning. *Journal of Clinical Psychology, 64*(10), 1145-1163.

Kotz, D. (2007, August). The right Rx for sadness. *US News and World Report, 143*(4). Retrieved from https://ehis.ebscohost.com/eds/detail?vid=12&hid=2&sid=729d1d)c-14b6-469f-a3

Klass, D., Silverman, P., & Nickman, S. (Eds.). (1996). *Continuing bonds: New understandings of grief.* Philadelphia, PA: Taylor & Francis.

Kubler-Ross, E. (1969). *On death and dying.* New York, NY: Macmillan.

Lifton, R.J. & Olson, E. (1976). The human meaning of total disaster: The Buffalo Creek experience. *Psychiatry, 39:* 1-18.

Lindemann, E. (1944). The symptomatology and management of acute grief. *American Journal of Psychiatry, 101,* 141-148.

Lynch, T. (1997). *The undertaking: Life studies from the dismal trade.* New York, NY: W.W. Norton.

Malkinson, R. & Bar-Tur, L. (2005). Long term bereavement processes of older parents: The three phases of grief. *OMEGA, 50*(2), 103-129.

Mancini, A.D. & Bonanno, G.A. (2006). Resilience in the face of potential trauma: Clinical practices and illustrations. *Journal of Clinical Psychology: In session, 62* (8), 971-985.

Mandelbaum, D.G. (1959). Social uses of funeral rites. In H. Feifel (Ed.), *The meaning of death* (pp. 58-75). New York, NY: McGraw-Hill.

Meagher, D.K. (2007). Ethical and legal issues and loss, grief, and mourning. In D. Balk, W. Cogrin, G. Thornton, & D. Meagher (Eds.), *Handbook of thanatology.* Northbrook, IL: Association for Death Education and Counseling.

Mellor, P.A. & Schilling, C. (1993). Modernity, self-identity, and the sequestration of death. *Sociology 27*(3), 411-431.

Mermann, A.C. (1992). Spiritual aspects of the dying. *Yale Journal of Biology and Medicine, 65,* 137-142.

Middleton, W., Burnett, P., Raphael, B., & Martinek, N. (1996). The bereavement response: A cluster analysis. *The British Journal of Psychiatry, 169*(2), 167-171.

Morgan, J.D. (1993). Existential quest for meaning. In K.J. Doka & J.D. Morgan (Eds.), *Death and spirituality* (pp. 3-12). Amityville, NY: Baywood Publishing.

National Center for Health Statistics. (2011). *Health, United States, 2011: With special feature on socioeconomic status and health.* Hyattsville, MD: Author. Retrieved from http://www.cdc.gove/nchs/data/hus11.pdf#summary

Parkes, C.M. (1998). Helping the bereaved I & II. In C. Parkes (Ed.), *Bereavement: Studies of grief in adult life* (3rd Ed., pp. 161-198). Madison, WI: International Universities Press.

Parkes, C.M., Laungani, P., & Young, B. (Eds.). (1997). A good introduction to the different cultural and religious beliefs and rituals around death and afterlife. In *Death and bereavement across cultures* (pp. 209-246). London, England: Routledge.

Parkes, C.M. & Weiss, R.S. (1983). *Recovery from bereavement.* New York, NY: Basic Books.

Parris, R.J. (2011). Initial management of bereaved relatives following trauma. *Trauma, 14*(2), 139-155.

Pasternak, R.E., Reynolds, C.F., Schlernitzauer, M., Hoch, C.C., Buysse, D.J., Houck, P.R., Perel, J.M. (1991). Acute open-trial nortirptyline therapy of bereavement-related depression in later life. *Journal of Clinical Psychiatry, 52*, 307-310.

Pelligrino, E.D. (2000). Decisions to withdraw life-sustaining treatment: A moral algorithm. *Journal of the American Medical Association, 283*(8), 1065-1067.

Phillips, B.J. (2005). Determining brain death: A summary. *The Internet Journal of Law, Healthcare and Ethics, 2*(2). doi: 10.5580/1f0a

Pine, V.R. (1995). Funerals: Life's final ceremonies. In B. Corless, B.B. Germino, & M.A. Pittman (Eds.), *A challenge for living: Dying, death, and bereavement* (pp. 99-116). Boston, MA: Jones and Bartlett.

Pine, V.R. (1969). Comparative funeral practices. *Practical Anthropology, 16*, 49-62.

President's Commission for the Study of Ethical Problems in Medicine and Behavioral Research (1981). *Defining death: A report on the medical, legal, and ethical issues in the determination of death.* Washington, DC: Government Printing Office.

Rainer, J.P. & Martin, J.C. (2013). *Isolated and alone: Therapeutic interventions for loneliness.* Sarasota, FL: Professional Resource Press.

Rando, T.A. (1984). *Grief, dying, and death: Clinical interventions for caregivers.* Champaign, IL: Research Press.

Rosenblatt, P.C. (2003). Bereavement in cross-cultural perspective. In C.D. Bryant (Ed.), *Handbook of death and dying: The response to death* (Vol. 2, pp. 596-624). Thousand Oaks, CA: Sage.

Rosenblatt, P.C. (2008). Recovery following bereavement: Metaphor, phenomenology, and culture. *Death Studies, 32*, 6-16.

Rosenblatt, P.C. (2008). Grief across cultures. In M.S. Stroebe, R.O. Hansson, W. Stroebe, & H. Schut (Eds.), *Handbook of bereavement research: Consequences, coping, and care* (pp. 423-450). Washington, DC: American Psychological Association.

Sanders, C.M. (1989). *Grief: The mourning after: Dealing with adult bereavement.* Oxford, England: Wiley.

Sanders, C.M. (1967). *Care of the dying: The management of terminal illness.* London, England: Hospital Medical Publications.

Sbarra, D.A., & Hazan, C. (2008). Coregulation, dysregulation, self-regulation: An integrative analysis and empirical agenda for understanding adult attachment, separation, loss, and recovery. *Personality and Social Psychology Review, 12*(2), 141-167.

Schneiderman, L.J., Jecker, N.S., & Jonsen, A.R. (1996). Medical futility: Response to critiques. *Annals of Internal Medicine, 125*(8), 669-674.

Shand, A.F. (1920). *The foundations of character.* London, U.K.: Macmillan.

Shapiro, E.R. (1994). *Grief as a family process.* New York, NY: Guilford.

Shear, M.K. (2011). Bereavement and the DSM5. *OMEGA, 64*(2), 101-118.

Shuter, P., Edwards, H., & Sacre, S. (2008). *Exploring grief and bereavement among family caregivers of people with severe dementia.* Paper presented at 8th International Conference on Grief and Bereavement in Contemporary Society, Melbourne, Australia.

Silverman, E., Range, L., & Overholser, J. (1995). Bereavement from suicide as compared to other forms of bereavement. *OMEGA, 30,* 41-51.

Steiner, C.S. (2006). Grief support groups used by few–are bereavement needs being met? *Journal of Social Work in End-of-Life and Palliative Care, 2*(1), 29-54.

Sternberg, R.J. (1986). A triangular theory of love. *Psychological Review, 93*(2), 119-135. doi:10.1037/0033-295X.93.2.119

Sterns, C.Z. (1993). Sadness. In M.L. Weid & J.M. Haviland (Eds.), *Handbook of emotions* (pp. 547-561). New York, NY: Guilford Press.

Stroebe, M.S., Hansson, R.O., Stroebe, W., & Schut, H. (Eds.). (2008). *Handbook of bereavement research: Consequences, coping, and care.* Washington, DC: American Psychological Association.

Stroebe, M.S. & Schut, H. (1999). The dual process model of coping with bereavement: Rationale and description. *Death Studies, 23*(3), 197-224.

Snyder, C.H. (1994). *The psychology of hope: You can get here from there.* New York, NY: Free Press.

Union Pacific Co. v. Botsford, 141 U.S. 250 (1891).

Weisman, A. (1972). *On dying and denying: A psychiatric study of terminality.* New York, NY: Behavioral Publications.

Vachon, M.L.S. & Stylianos, S.K. (1988). The role of social support in bereavement. *Journal of Social Issues, 44,* 175-190.

van der Houwen, K., Stroebe, M., Stroebe, W., Schut, H., van den Bout, S., & Wijngaardse-de Meij, L. (2010). Risk factors for bereavement outcome: A multivariate approach. *Death Studies, 34,* 195-220.

Volkan, V. (1975). Regrief therapy. In B. Schoenberg, I. Gerber, A. Wiener, A. H. Kutscher, D. Peretz, & A.C. Carr (Eds.), *Bereavement: Its psychosocial aspects* (pp. 43-66). New York, NY: Columbia University Press.

Welshons, J. (2002). *Awakening from grief.* Maplewood, NJ: Open Heart Publications.

Wolfelt, A.D. (1998). Companioning vs. treating: Beyond the medical model of bereavement caregiving: Part 3. *The Forum Newsletter.* Association of Death Education and Counseling.

Worden, W. (1982). *Grief counseling and therapy: A handbook for the mental health practitioner.* New York, NY: Springer.

Zisook, S., Corruble, E., Duan, N., Iglewicz, A., Karam, E.G., Lanuoette, N., & Young, I.T. (2012). The bereavement exclusion and DSM-5. *Depression & Anxiety, 29*(5), 425-443.

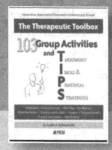

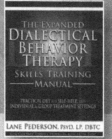